EDUCATION MATTERS

General Editor: Professor Ted Wragg

EDUCATING THE UNDER-FIVES

BOOKS IN THIS SERIES

Vocational Education and Training *by Pat Ainley*

Managing Finance in Schools *by Tim Blanchard, Bob Lovell and Nick Ville*

Higher Education *by Donald Bligh*

Growth in Children *by John Brierley*

Testing and Assessment *by Charles Desforges*

The Education of Girls *by Jane French*

Secondary Education *by Maureen O'Connor*

Schools and Parents *by John Partington and Ted Wragg*

Learning in Primary Schools *by Andrew Pollard*

The New Curriculum *by Richard Pring*

Special Education *by Jonathan Solity*

Drama in the Curriculum *by John Somers*

Adult Education *by Michael Stephens*

EDUCATING THE UNDER-FIVES

Elizabeth A. Smith

CASSELL

Cassell

Villiers House
41/47 Strand
London WC2N 5JE

387 Park Avenue South
New York
NY 10016–8810

British Library Cataloguing-in-Publication Data
A catalogue record for this book is available from the British Library.

ISBN: 0–304–32977–0 (hardback)
0–304–32975–4 (paperback)

Phototypeset by Intype, London
Printed and bound in Great Britain by
Biddles Ltd, Guildford and King's Lynn

CONTENTS

Foreword   vii

1 Past and present   1

2 The range of provision   18

3 Change and challenge   36

4 Problems and possibilities   51

5 Laying the foundations   63

6 A curriculum for the under-fives   80

7 Towards the twenty-first century   106

Bibliography   112

Appendix   116

Index   117

For my mother

FOREWORD

Professor E. C. Wragg, Exeter University

During the 1980s a succession of Education Acts changed considerably the nature of schools and their relationships with the outside world. Parents were given more rights and responsibilities, including the opportunity to serve on the governing body of their child's school. The 1988 Education Reform Act in particular, by introducing for the first time a National Curriculum, the testing of children at the ages of 7, 11, 14 and 16, local management, including financial responsibility and the creation of new types of school, was a radical break with the past. Furthermore the disappearance of millions of jobs, along with other changes in our society, led to reforms not only of schools, but also of further and higher education.

In the wake of such rapid and substantial changes it was not just parents and lay people, but also teachers and other professionals working in education, who found themselves struggling to keep up with what these many changes meant and how to get the best out of them. The *Education Matters* series addresses directly the major topics of reform, such as the new curriculum, testing and assessment, the role of parents and the handling of school finances, considering their effects on primary, secondary, further and higher education, and also the continuing education of adults.

The aim of the series is to present information about the challenges facing education in the remainder of the twentieth century in an authoritative but readable form. The books in the series, therefore, are of particular interest to parents, governors and all those concerned with education, but are written in such a way as to give an overview to students, experienced teachers and other professionals who work in the field.

Each book gives an account of the relevant legislation and background, but, more importantly, stresses practical implications of change with specific examples of what is being or can be done to make reforms work effectively. The authors are not only authorities in their field, but also have direct experience of the matters they write about. That is why the *Education Matters* series makes an important contri{zo both debate and practice.

Chapter 1

PAST AND PRESENT

The position of the youngest children in society has always been vulnerable. Responsibility for children lies predominantly within the family and it is up to individuals to make suitable arrangements for their children according to needs and circumstances. The involvement of the state, whether through health, education or social services, has tended to be on a selective basis, and has promoted a policy of protection from harm rather than one of widely available, publicly funded, high-quality provision as a right for young children.

Such an ideal has remained elusive for many reasons. The status of children in society, the state of the economy, political ideologies, changing patterns of family life and employment are all influential factors. These have conspired to create a disparate framework within which the development of cohesive, co-ordinated structures and services has been difficult to achieve. In terms of educating the under-fives, this has also helped to perpetuate inequity and inequality in the earliest years of life. During the twentieth century, the state has intervened in education for 5- to 16-year-olds with increasing and unprecedented powers whilst at the same time allowing the vagaries of the free market to make provision for the majority of young children.

The fragmented nature of provision for the under-fives has arisen over many decades. This has resulted in wide variations in the quality of education and experience in the first five years. The current system is wasteful and divisive and fails to meet the needs of children and their families. Successive governments, of whatever political persuasion, have failed to address these needs and problems, leaving a trail of unfulfilled promises and a chaotic system which compares unfavourably with most other countries in Europe.

A review of the evolution of provision will show several recurring themes which have been influential in determining the current state of affairs. The next section will outline the impact of legislation and chart significant trends against a background of social, political and economic change.

The historical background

In the nineteenth century, education was not available to all children as it is today. Those from wealthier families were educated by a governess or tutor, then in public or private schools. For children of 'the lower orders', elementary education was funded largely by charitable foundations. By the middle of the century about one in eleven children received some form of education in elementary schools or Sunday schools, often of dubious quality. Most children were denied any education, since they were expected to become economically productive at an early age and contribute to the family income in both rural and urban areas. Young babies were left at home to enable mothers to return to work as soon as possible. Care might be provided by an older child or family member or in a Dame School. These tended to be run by older women in the community and catered for anything up to forty or fifty children, often in cramped unsuitable conditions, particularly in urban areas.

Some pioneering work on behalf of children had been carried out by Robert Owen in the early part of the century. In 1816 he established what was effectively a workplace nursery-cum-factory school at his mills in New Lanark, Scotland – the Institution for the Formation of Character. As the name suggests, Owen believed that education in the early years helped to form future citizens, and that environmental factors were influential in this process. The children were allowed to indulge their 'naturalness' in play, dancing, music, nature study and painting. Owen's initiatives, funded by his company's profits, were not entirely philanthropic since he realized the benefits of such provision in terms of both allowing mothers to return to work and encouraging desirable habits and dispositions in the next generation of workers. He encouraged fellow mill-owners to devote the same care and attention to their workforce as they did to their machinery. However, since Owen was an atheist, a social reformer and a trade-unionist, his educational ideas and methods had little influence on state provision and were not copied to any extent by fellow industrialists.

For many children of the labouring classes, life was brutal. Often children as young as 4 or 5 were engaged for long hours in dangerous work. Bad living conditions, inadequate sanitation, overcrowding and undernourishment all contributed to a poor quality of life. For their parents, low and irregular earnings, particularly for women, were a cause of extreme poverty. Rates of infant mortality were high in the nineteenth century – one in six children died before their first birthday. The average life expectancy in 1850 was 45, but could be as low as 30 for the poor. They were middle-aged by their thirties, and well into old age by their forties, so there was precious little time for a long period of childhood.

In the last quarter of the nineteenth century attitudes towards children in society began to shift. The work of social reformers such as Charles Booth and Seebohm Rowntree highlighted the plight of the poor, whilst a better-educated, healthier workforce became paramount in Britain's need to retain competitiveness as other countries industrialized.

The Education Act of 1870 introduced compulsory school attendance for children from 'not less than five years' although in practice children below this age were not excluded. Babies' classes were common and by 1900, nearly 43 per cent (1.5 million) of children aged 3 to 5 years were attending elementary schools in England and Wales (Whitbread, 1972, p. 42). This type of provision was unsuitable, with the children sitting in rows on hard wooden benches, taught in large groups (up to a hundred), often with harsh physical punishments. It is difficult to imagine today how young, naturally energetic and inquisitive children could endure such conditions.

In 1905 the Board of Education separated nursery from elementary education, thus establishing state-funded provision for the under-fives and the official age of entry to statutory schooling. Pressure for greater government intervention in education and health had been increasing steadily with the continued work of the Edwardian social reformers. The Fabian Society added its voice to these demands. In a tract entitled 'The Endowment of Motherhood', H. D. Harben argued for primary health care, preventative medicine and childcare facilities at community level on the grounds that

> Money spent on the beginning of life is more economical than money spent at the end of life . . . It may be regarded as an investment bearing interest in the shape of health, energy, intelligence and labour power in the coming generation. It is financially well worth our while to develop our children, or at least to safeguard them sufficiently to enable them to accomplish the work that lies before them in life. (1910, p. 4)

The welfare reforms of the Liberal government in 1906 had already introduced school meals for 'needy' children as well as medical inspection for all school children. A falling birth rate meant that children were increasingly an asset to the nation and, as such, had to be safeguarded accordingly. However, as expenditure increased on statutory schooling, the under-fives were seen as less of a priority. The needs of children were still clearly bound up with the needs of the economy and society and, as will be shown later in this book, the arguments presented then were being repeated eighty years later.

The relationship between child welfare and education was clearly established by this time, although for the under-fives the emphasis tended to be more on the former than on the latter. There was now a more fertile ground for the ideas of educational theorists, philosophers and practitioners in the field of early childhood education. Throughout the 1920s and 1930s the pioneering work of Rachel and Margaret McMillan, Maria Montessori and Susan Isaacs became increasingly influential, as did the ideas of Friedrich Froebel and Rudolf Steiner (Bruce, 1987; Anning, 1991).

The McMillan sisters were both philanthropists. Margaret was a political activist and campaigned vigorously for the provision of schools and health care, particularly in the slum districts. By 1915 nine out of ten children survived their first year of life, but those in the poorest homes were still most vulnerable to disease and infections. The McMillans believed in the benefits of good diet, cleanliness, sunlight and fresh air – particularly in view of the incidence of tuberculosis and other infectious diseases in the densely populated urban areas. Their primary concerns were with children's health and they set up a clinic in Deptford in 1910 which catered for around 6000 children a year. These gradually developed into camp schools, and a baby camp was opened in 1914 (Steedman, 1990, p. 90).

Margaret used her experience and ideals to establish nursery schools, based on similar principles. The nurseries were homely, largely informal and stimulating places where children were allowed to choose between a variety of activities. The classrooms were connected by long open-air verandahs, with a large nursery garden which McMillan thought to be essential. Liaison with parents and the education of mothers were also seen as important. In 1914, Margaret wrote:

> In the evening a crowd of mothers used to come. They wandered about the garden. They gathered in the shelter. They looked at the bathing and dressing, feeding and play. Space at last. Fellowship at last, and under the open sky! (Steedman, 1990, p. 990)

The McMillan nurseries provided a blueprint in terms of both architecture and practice for many years to come. Their ideas and those of Montessori, Isaacs and Froebel were influential in the recommendations of the Board of Education's Consultative Committee on Infant and Nursery Schools (1933). One of the recommendations stated, 'We regard the provision of open shelters, with a liberal space for a garden-playground, as an essential feature in the design of all newly provided nursery schools' (p. 106).

5

The work of the McMillans also exemplified certain trends in the care and education of the under-fives which continued throughout the twentieth century: the interrelationship between health, welfare and education; the importance of parent education; the need for appropriate provision for young children and their families at a local level and a spirit of fellowship and community, particularly for women. Most of their pioneering work was funded from private and charitable donations, with state involvement increasing only after the First World War.

Although most provision was targeted at children from poorer families and deprived backgrounds, the benefits of nursery education were being recognized by middle-class and professional families whose children were normally looked after by home-based nannies. In 1928, four middle-class parents started an open-air nursery school in Chelsea which revealed a different kind of deprivation:

> It took months to train children who had had nannies to be independent in dressing, washing and use of the lavatory. Their teacher noticed that 'the children at this nursery school were more talkative than in slum nursery schools, but less interested in making use of the environment furnished'. They were accordingly nicknamed the 'Kensington Cripples'. (Whitbread, 1972, p. 72)

Again this type of provision was available only to the few and, as state funding for the statutory elementary and secondary sectors increased, additional resources for the under-fives were not forthcoming. Under the 1918 Education Act, provision for 2- to 5-year-olds was made non-statutory and was left to the discretion of individual local authorities. Thus began the long tradition in Britain of significant local variations in the levels of provision in the maintained sector. By this time only 15.3 per cent of under-fives had places in any form of maintained school and the compensatory nature of much provision was continued. This position was again reflected in the Board of Education's Report (1933):

> We fully recognise ... that the home surroundings of large numbers of children are not satisfactory and we think that children

below the age of five from such homes might with great benefit to themselves, to their parents, and to the State, attend either separate nursery schools or nursery classes within public elementary schools. (p. 114)

The next significant state-funded impetus to expanded provision came during the Second World War as women were drawn into the workforce to replace men and boost war production. By 1944 there was a peak of 70,000 places in day nurseries, but this figure was already beginning to decline by the end of the war. As men returned from the services, women were expected to return to their primary function as homemakers and mothers. The influence of the work of John Bowlby, an American psychologist, was also formative in this process. He argued that mothers were the primary, essential caregivers and that early separation of young babies and children resulted in maternal deprivation.

The 1944 Education Act is regarded as a landmark for introducing secondary education for all. It also required local authorities to plan with regard to the need

for securing that provision is made for pupils who have not attained the age of five years by the provision of nursery schools or, where the authority consider the provision of such schools to be inexpedient, by the provision of nursery classes in other schools. (Whitbread, 1972, p. 110)

At the time this seemed to be an optimistic statement of intent, although provision was still discretionary rather than mandatory. The expansion of secondary education and, subsequently, higher education proved expensive and the hoped-for increase in state-funded nursery education did not occur.

In 1945 a joint policy statement by the Ministries of Health and Education established some fundamental principles which shaped post-war attitudes and provision. Children under 2 should be cared for at home, the number of day nursery places should be reduced, and remaining provision should be allocated to 2- to 5-year-olds. In addition, places should be reserved for children whose mothers were 'constrained by individual circumstances to go out to work or whose home conditions are themselves unsatisfactory from the health point of view, or whose mothers are incapable for some good reason of undertaking the full care of their children' (Garland and White, 1980, p. 4). Three years later, the official age of entry to statutory schooling was fixed at the term before children reached their fifth birthday. The infant and junior phases were combined as the first stage in statutory education, thus marginalizing nursery provision.

The above statement reinforced prevailing attitudes about the place of women in society and their responsibilities to their children. It also established a clear link between children in need and access to provision. By 1966, the number of places in day nurseries had declined markedly to around 21,000 and did not meet demand. It was left increasingly to private and voluntary organizations to fill the gaps left by the state sector.

The weak political and economic position of provision for the under-fives was clearly entrenched by this time. In 1967, the Central Advisory Council for Education (Plowden Report) stated that nursery education on a large scale remained an unfulfilled promise and recommended that there should be nursery places available for all children whose parents wished them to attend from the age of 3. Although this was a laudable statement in itself, it referred only to maintained provision for 3- to 5-year-olds and did not acknowledge the need for flexibility, choice and diversity for all under-fives.

In 1972 the Conservative government published a White Paper entitled *A Framework for Expansion* which accepted the Plowden Report's recommendation on the expansion of nursery education. However, the increase in provision did not occur on the scale intended due to the oil crisis and economic recession. This again showed the dependency of provision on the state of the national economy. What expansion did take place tended to be concentrated in the Educational Priority Areas. These were designated areas, mainly in large inner cities and urban conurbations, which received additional funding in order to compensate for the effects of poverty, overcrowding and living in high-rise tower blocks.

This was very much in line with the educational thinking of the day, which advocated compensatory education. Research carried out here and in America examined the influence of heredity, environment and social conditions on intelligence and educational attainment. It was believed that the effects of social deprivation could be remedied or at least alleviated by early intervention. Again it was stressed that investment in pre-school education could be justified on the basis of potentially greater benefits to society and the economy through a better-educated workforce. The relationship between compensatory education, deprivation and social need was still a dominant factor in determining provision.

As provision became more tightly focused upon defined need, other changes were taking place which began to force the issue of childcare for the under-fives higher on to the political and economic agenda. During the 1970s, a fall in the birth rate meant that there were fewer teenage school leavers available to enter the workplace. At the same time, heavy industries were beginning to contract and were being increasingly replaced by jobs in the retail and service sectors – finance, leisure, hotels and catering, i.e. women's jobs. This meant that women were being encouraged back into the workplace and the demand for childcare rose accordingly. It was soon apparent that existing state-funded provision simply could not meet these demands. Places in local-authority day nurseries were allocated in relation to a defined need. Nursery schools and classes mostly provided part-time places and their hours did not coincide with parents' needs. Private nurseries were expensive, workplace nurseries were few and far between. Childminders, who have always provided the flexibility required by working parents, fulfilled some of the demand, with places increasing from 88,000 in 1975 to 139,000 in 1985. However, this form of provision is expensive and is not necessarily an option for those in lower-income brackets.

Clearly, the needs of the economy were at odds with the needs of young children and their families and, by the 1980s, there was an emerging crisis in the provision of childcare. This became inextricably bound up with debates about the responsibilities of parents, women's rights to work, the relative roles of the state and employers, costs and benefits. The British government took a firmly *laissez-faire* stance, preferring to leave demand and supply to market forces. Again this left the under-fives vulnerable in many different ways. The demand for female labour and women's rights issues seemed to be taking precedence over the debate about appropriate forms of provision for young children and indeed about their rights. It became evident that key issues needed to be addressed swiftly if the needs and interests of children were to be safeguarded in the climate of the time.

Increasingly the debate about the provision of childcare was not just about quantity but about quality. In 1988 the British government ordered an inquiry by the Education, Science and Arts Committee (ESAC) into Educational Provision for the Under-Fives. Its brief was to focus on education rather than the whole range of services for the under-fives, and it concentrated predominantly on 3- and 4-year-olds. However, its findings and recommendations had wider implications, as did the response of the Conservative government.

The report emphasized the need for a wider policy of expansion. It considered care and education to be inseparable and essential to good-quality provision. However, it also reinforced the notion that where local authorities made provision for this age group, and where places were scarce, priority should be given to those with greatest need. The report noted the possibility that provision might become dominated by children

> who are given places for one special reason or another instead of allowing a proper balance to develop between all groups of children. If a balance is not maintained then the full educational experience will not be available to all and there is a danger that some form of social stigma will attach to attendance. (4.27, p. xix)

Another recurrent theme was the need for nursery education to demonstrate its effectiveness. It was noted that higher education, industrial training for 16- to 19-year-olds, adult education and the requirements of the National Curriculum would all 'swallow up additional money to good effect. So nursery education has to make a very strong case' (2.8, p. viii). The implication here was that nursery education could not demonstrate the same returns and was a bolt-on extra rather than a real necessity, in spite of mounting evidence from Britain and the United States about the long-term beneficial effects of pre-school provision. However, the report did make a strong case for co-ordination of services for the under-fives, improved liaison between the service providers, improved status and training for all under-five workers and increased public expenditure.

The response given by the DES on behalf of the Conservative government was very much in line with the political ideology of the day, which placed increasing emphasis on reducing public-sector expenditure and on encouraging individual responsibility and private-sector involvement.

> The Government will continue to accord appropriate priority to provision for young children, while recognising that precedence may have to be given to expenditure required to bring about the introduction of the major reforms of education . . . set by the Education Reform Act 1988. The Government also believes that there is substantial scope for private and voluntary sector involvement in this field, and will seek ways of maximising the contribution which such provision can make to the fulfilment of demand for high quality nursery education. (ESAC First Special Report, 5, p. 1)

This report coincided with a review of services for the under-fives carried out in 1988 by the National Children's Bureau. This revealed some fundamental concerns which echoed trends and attitudes inherited from the past. Services were fragmented and uncoordinated, with wide regional variations in the quantity of provision available. There was a continued absence of a national policy on the under-fives and a low commitment to developing and resourcing pre-school services. The report raised questions about what should be provided and by whom and also noted the seemingly intractable problems that would have to be surmounted in order to establish a clear sense of direction and achieve real progress. The review concluded that coherent local policies within the context of an overall national strategy were needed urgently (Pugh, 1988, p. 82). The debate about organization and structures also needed to be informed by broader considerations such as the balance between care and education, the quality of children's lives and experiences, accountability and standards in the different settings.

The care/education divide had been a long-standing feature of provision for the under-fives. Its origins can be traced back to the nineteenth century and even the work of the McMillan sisters reinforced the notion that deprived children needed to be restored physically before they could be stimulated mentally. Day nurseries tended to continue this emphasis on care, nurture and protection and regarded their role as providing stability, security and some compensation for children in need. They were less concerned with children's development from an educational point of view.

A study carried out by Parry and Archer noted that the staff in day nurseries were often overly occupied with the many practical chores involved in their work and although there was evidence of warmth and empathy, there was 'insufficient understanding of the children's intellectual needs' (1974, p. 44). The emphasis on welfare and the compensatory nature of provision were also evident in some of the nursery schools and classes in this study.

> By the very nature of the social catchment area of some of the schools, a choice of priorities had to be made between the nurture, care and intellectual needs of the children. (1974, p. 7)

These commitments are revealing about not just different practices and priorities, but also social attitudes and prevailing ideas about early learning and development. It was also the case that such attitudes were entrenched within the different service providers. Those in Health and Social Services were as defensive about children's welfare as those in Education were about their cognitive development. The ESAC Report (1988) recommended closer liaison between the different service providers, with teachers to be employed in day nurseries and the expertise of the educational advisory service to be used. The response of the Association of Metropolitan Authorities was guarded. 'Some authorities are cautious about subjugating the "care" and social/emotional development work of day nurseries to educational provision' (ESAC, 1989, 27, p. 14).

Although the best nurseries had always provided care and education, over the years it has been to the detriment of children that the two were seen as divisible and distinct. The care/education divide also left a legacy of structural, practical and philosophical problems to be addressed. All three sector providers, Health, Education and Social Services, had their own priorities and interests to uphold, particular purposes and practices to defend, different strategies for management and organization, established training, career paths and hierarchies. By the late 1980s these factors were contributing to continued entrenchment and confusion in policies and practices. Whilst there was considerable diversity in provision, this did not automatically imply choice and certainly did not guarantee quality.

Gradually, the pressure for change and development increased for several reasons. Existing structures and practices were shown to be inadequate and insufficient to meet the needs of children and their parents, as well as employers. Research evidence from the United States continued to demonstrate long-lasting benefits to children and to society as a whole of high-quality pre-school education. Research studies revealed important insights into the lives and experiences of children in different pre-school settings, and added considerably to the knowledge base in early childhood education. There was greater awareness and organization on the part of children's pressure groups, which started to take on a more active political role. The issue of children's rights was also raised on to the political agenda. In addition the last quarter of the twentieth century witnessed significant changes in family life and structure, the distribution of wealth, and in patterns of employment, all of which brought into focus some fundamental issues about the rights and responsibilities of individuals and the state.

In relation to the under-fives, two reports focused attention on the quality of education received by 3- to 5-year-olds. These were followed by the Children Act 1989, which had major implications for the future direction and development of services for this age group. *The Education of Children under Five* (DES, 1989) examined maintained provision in nursery schools and classes and in reception classes in primary schools. The report identified aspects of good practice and outlined a model of curriculum organization based on nine areas of learning and experience (DES, 1985) and incorporating play. This supported the view that there was such a thing as a curriculum for this age group. It stressed the importance of breadth, balance, relevance, progression and continuity, but also made several key recommendations as to how these might be achieved: more early years teachers trained for this age group; improved training for teachers and nursery nurses; better facilities and accommodation and better adult/child ratios.

These recommendations were endorsed by the Committee of Inquiry chaired by Angela Rumbold, then Minister of State at the DES with responsibility for the under-fives (DES, 1990). This committee had a wider brief and examined the diversity of needs and types of provision. This was an insightful report which again made some important recommendations for policy makers, local-authority providers and practitioners. It looked at key aspects of quality control, curriculum, staffing and training and identified a range of essential needs:

> ... a closer linkage between the three strands of health, care and education in initial and in-service training; a pattern of vocational training and qualifications for childcare workers which will bridge the gap between vocational and academic qualifications; safeguarding both the rigour and relevance of initial training for the under-fives; and affording improved opportunities of in-service training for childcare workers in educational settings.

Both these reports gave clear guidelines for how quality might be achieved through policy and practice across the different settings. The Rumbold Report called for a clear lead from central government in setting a national framework within which local developments could take place (215, p. 29). It also recommended that local authority providers should 'establish and promulgate clear quality criteria for all services in their area which take full account of the requirements for all under-fives, including those with special needs, and for those for whom English is a second language' (230a, p. 31).

These two reports were followed by the Children Act 1989 which was implemented in 1991. This introduced major legislative changes which had far-reaching implications for children, parents, service providers, legal systems and children's rights. The impact of the Act on services for children under 5 will be examined in more detail later in this book. At this point it is important to note that the Act, along with the reports noted above, seemed to offer significant hope of progress and improvements for young children in the quantity and quality of the services offered. By the early 1990s, there were clear guidelines and structures for future development, and the needs of the under-fives and their families were being given due consideration and recognition.

However, what became clear was the enormity of the task facing local authorities in complying with the terms of the Act. The organizational and administrative tasks alone were onerous, let alone the responsibility for establishing quality criteria, registering and inspecting all provision for the under-fives, and ensuring their compliance with those criteria. The Act demanded new ways of working which required the breaking down of barriers between departments, setting aside professional jealousies and territorial influence, establishing a common language and frameworks for future development, including multi-professional, inter-disciplinary training.

Inevitably perhaps, in view of the previous history of the status of the under-fives, insufficient funds were made available to support the necessary changes. Once again competing initiatives, as well as ideological priorities on the part of the Conservative government, worked against the innovative reforms of the Children Act. Increasingly its terms were interpreted as prioritizing a welfare service for children in need rather than promoting entitlement to high-quality provision for all. Again there were tensions between funding priorities for the under-fives in particular, and for the under-eights in general.

The Education Reform Act of 1988 (ERA) had committed massive government expenditure to support its implementation over a number of years. The requirements for testing children at 7 had raised questions about 'baseline' testing of children at 5 or on entry to primary school. Changes were also made to the way in which schools were funded, and how those funds were managed. Budgets were allocated on the basis of formula funding, and were devolved to individual schools under the Local Management of Schools (LMS) initiative. Schools were encouraged to take on the free-market ethos and, with open enrolment, to compete for pupils since each pupil brought in a certain income, according to age. This helped to support the rise in the number of 4-year-olds entering reception classes early. The appropriateness of such provision was questioned by educationalists on several grounds, particularly since it was regarded as nursery education on the cheap. However, much provision for 4-year-olds in school was not based upon good nursery practice. All too often, younger children were admitted without adequate planning, resourcing or due consideration of their needs (Bennett and Kell, 1989; Cleave and Brown, 1991).

It was clear, even in the early 1990s, that building a consensus for future developments based on adequate funding and prioritization was still an uphill struggle. Whilst the Children Act, the Rumbold Report and greater advocacy for young children seemed to offer hope, other changes, particularly local government reforms, local financial management of schools, cutbacks in public expenditure, rising unemployment and economic recession pointed to a more negative view. As long as provision and services for the under-fives remained non-statutory, they remained vulnerable. In addition, whilst so much diversity existed between the different settings in terms of qualifications, training, aims and purposes, a higher quality of educational experience for all under-fives seemed likely to remain an elusive ideal.

In spite of this, there were optimistic signs that local and national pressure groups and local authorities were doing what they could within limited and limiting means. It has always been the case that lack of political will at a national level can, to a certain extent, be compensated for by a ground-swell of activity and commitment at a local level. As noted above, local authorities faced a demanding task in complying with the requirements of the Children Act. In order to understand the complexity of the under-fives muddle, the next chapter will give a detailed outline of the different forms of provision and will examine issues relating to co-ordination, resourcing, staffing and training.

Chapter 2

THE RANGE OF PROVISION

In Great Britain, there are three main sector providers:

1. Public Sector – government-funded;
2. Voluntary Sector – government-funded and fee-paying;
3. Private Sector – fee-paying.

At a national level, three government departments are involved with the under-fives:

1. Department for Education
2. Department of Health
3. Department of Social Services

At a regional level, four local government departments are involved with the under-fives:

1. Local Education Authorities
2. Social Services Departments
3. Area Health Authorities
4. Leisure Departments

All have different priorities, objectives, philosophies and values. Frequently their areas of influence and involvement overlap but this has not always fostered good working relationships, co-ordination or communication. Each department has its own budget and makes decisions about how funds will be allocated according to needs and priorities. This means that budgets, territories and power have tended to be jealously guarded. We have already seen how the traditional divide between care and education has resulted in a two-tier system which has not necessarily been in the best interests of children. In addition, staff come from a variety of training backgrounds and may have different views about what is appropriate for young children, and what should take precedence. These factors have all been influential in shaping the continuing under-fives muddle at the level of policy and practice.

In order to consider how provision and services for the under-fives might develop in the future, it is necessary to describe their current form, purposes and objectives. The next section will give a brief summary of provision within the three main sector providers (Penn and Riley, 1992, p. 20). This will be followed by a detailed examination of each type of provision, with statistical information about rates of participation. The adult:child ratios and the qualifications required are those specified in the Children Act (1989).

1. Public Sector
This includes a wide range of provision funded separately or jointly across the three government departments. It is maintained but non-statutory:

Nursery schools and classes, under-fives in reception classes in primary schools, special schools, Portage schemes, day nurseries, family centres, combined nursery centres, One O'clock Clubs.

2. Voluntary Sector
This includes voluntary groups, childcare organizations and children's charitable foundations:

Playgroups, family centres and family-support services, toy libraries, after-school clubs, parent and toddler groups.

3. Private Sector
This includes all forms of provision which are a private arrangement between the parent and the service provider:

Childminders, nannies, private day nurseries, workplace nurseries, independent schools.

Overview of provision

Public-sector provision

Nursery schools and classes

Some local authorities have provided nursery schools and classes for the under-fives, predominantly for 3- to 5-year-olds. Provision is non-statutory – at the discrimination of individual authorities – but is within the maintained sector, and varies between different areas of the country. For example, in 1992, amongst the lowest providers of maintained nursery education were Gloucestershire, 0 per cent; Bromley 2 per cent; Havering 4 per cent; and Dorset 5 per cent. The best providers were Wolverhampton 70 per cent; Newham 58 per cent; Merton and Cleveland 57 per cent; and Manchester 55 per cent.

Attendance is predominantly part-time, usually between 2 and 2½ hours per session for five half days per week. This means that even where available it is not always feasible for working parents. Fees are not charged and places are allocated either on a first-come-first-served basis or to children who have been identified as being in need, depending on local circumstances.

Nursery schools have their own headteacher, nursery classes are attached to primary schools. Both are staffed by trained teachers and nursery nurses at a ratio of around 1:13. Demand for places tends to outstrip supply since British nursery education is widely regarded as providing good practice. In 1992, there were 630,000 children in England below compulsory school age in maintained nursery and primary schools. Of these, 330,000 (52 per cent) were in nursery schools and classes (DES 11/93).

Reception classes

The statutory age of entry to primary schools is 5. Traditionally, schools had three termly intakes of children according to the date of their fifth birthday, although some authorities preferred a twice-yearly entrance in September and January.

However, with falling rolls schools began to change their admission policies, producing a three-tier system. Some maintained the original pattern of two or three intakes, whilst others adopted a policy of one intake for all 'rising fives' in September. Intake procedures also vary between staggered entry, part-time provision for the first few weeks leading to full-time provision, or full-time from the outset. Whether these procedures are in the interests of the children, the school or parents is debatable.

The early-entry policy means that children who are only just 4 are starting at primary school, often without due consideration for their needs and characteristics, usually with much higher pupil/teacher ratios than in other under-fives settings. It is up to each local authority to determine what staffing levels are appropriate in particular cases. This has resulted in significant variations, with some classes as high as 1:36. Teachers may have a nursery nurse or classroom assistant attached for some or all of the time but this is not compulsory and has forced many teachers to rely on parental help.

In 1992 55 per cent (347,000) of children aged 4 at the beginning of the school year were admitted to maintained primary schools during the autumn term – all of them below compulsory school age. The number of pupils in maintained nursery and primary provision has increased by 4 per cent (26,000) since 1991, and by 43 per cent (172,000) since 1983. However, much of this increase has been accounted for by the early-entry policy. Considerable concern has been voiced about this trend, in terms of a shortage of staff trained for this age group, the higher pupil/teacher ratios permissible in reception classes, the lack of facilities and equipment, and the need to provide a curriculum appropriate to this age group. Children are not always admitted into classes which are exclusively for their age and may be with 5- to 7-year-olds depending on organization within individual schools. The introduction of the National Curriculum and testing at 7 raised anxieties about reception classes becoming too formal too soon, with a 'top-down' approach and consequent undervaluing of play. Early entry is no substitute for nursery education. In spite of these reservations, the policy has proved popular with parents.

Local-authority day nurseries

These are run by Social Services and have traditionally emphasized care rather than education. Children between 0 and 5 years of age are catered for, many of whom are referred by health and social workers as being in need or at risk. The 'in need' criteria covers a range of problems, including special educational needs, children experiencing stress, behavioural problems, unsatisfactory home conditions, family illness or breakdown. Children 'at risk' are considered to be in danger of neglect, physical, sexual or emotional abuse. One disadvantage of day nurseries is their concentration of children with difficulties and the possible attachment of social stigma to attendance.

These nurseries open for longer hours and offer full- or part-time care. They are staffed by nursery nurses and care assistants. Fees are charged but are usually means-tested – based on parents' ability to pay. The standard recommended ratios for all day-care establishments are: 0 to 2 years 1:3; 2 to 3 years 1:4; 3 to 5 years 1:8. At least half the staff should be qualified in day care, early years education or social work. Officers in charge and their deputies should hold a relevant qualification in childcare, early years education, social work, health visiting or children's nursing.

As with day nurseries in the past, many of the children attending may lead difficult and fractured lives. The levels of stress can cause emotional and behavioural difficulties, presenting staff with additional challenges. In the past, compensating for disadvantage was seen as more important than educational stimulation. However, for these children further disadvantage could be caused by not giving appropriate educational input. These factors have clear implications for the training of staff and curriculum development.

Recent trends have seen shifts towards a broader, more balanced approach, including better liaison with parents and parentcraft classes. The Children Act 1989 requires that all day-care settings should offer experiences compatible in quality with those in nursery schools or classes. Day-care nurseries cater for 1 per cent of children under 5.

Family centres

Family Centres fulfil a range of functions and focus on the child and the family. Parents can obtain information about nutrition, health care, family planning, local-authority services and benefits. Some run parentcraft and adult-education classes as well as local support groups. Parents also have access to health and community workers. Family Centres run by Social Services Departments have the same staffing ratios and training requirements as day-care nurseries. The amount of childcare provided is variable. Some also provide after-school and holiday care for older children as well.

Combined centres

These are jointly funded and managed by Education and Social Services and are run by trained nursery nurses and teachers, each with their own lines of management. They were established in the early 1970s, mostly in educational priority areas, and aimed to combine the best elements of day care and education. The intention was to create a more broadly based, flexible service. Places were allocated to a broader cross-section of children in the local community, not just those at risk or in need, to create a less stigmatized service.

They offer full- or part-time care and open for up to fifty weeks a year. Hours are usually longer – from seven or eight o'clock in the morning till five or six o'clock at night. As with day nurseries, children are referred on the basis of need and fees are charged according to means. Many offer a range of support services for parents including after-school care for primary-age children and adult-education classes. Adult/child ratios are the same as for day nurseries. Staff are required to have a balance of skills and qualifications in early years teaching, nursery nursing or childcare. At least 50 per cent of the staff should be qualified.

Combined centres brought together staff from different traditions and training backgrounds. As Ferri *et al.* noted (1981, p. 198), the challenge was formidable in terms of changing attitudes and well-established practices and of relinquishing jealousy guarded areas of control. This was not always helped by lack of communication between Social Services and Education departments.

The staff also had different perceptions of their aims and purposes. Because of this, working relationships were sometimes difficult, with the staff unsure about their roles. However, this in itself meant that solutions and ways forward were sought. The lessons learnt from these experiences have provided a valuable blueprint for the development of interdisciplinary, multi-professional co-operation, particularly in the light of the requirements of the Children Act.

Special schools

Children under 5 with statements of special educational need may be catered for in any of the previous settings according to the nature of their needs and disabilities. Some have places in special schools. These are funded jointly between Education, Health and Social Services and may have additional input from charitable organizations. The teachers who staff them often have additional qualifications in special education needs, and there are nursery nurses and care assistants.

Children and their families have access to specialists in child development – educational psychologists, physiotherapists, speech therapists, orthoptists, audiologists and paediatricians. Additional home-based support may also be given by health visitors, home-visiting teachers and/or Portage workers. Other support services available, depending on need, include child guidance, mental handicap development team, social services, ophthalmologist, child psychiatrist, dietician and dentist.

The children's statements are reviewed and updated regularly so that decisions can be made as to the best type of placement when they reach the age of 5 and what support will be needed. The policy of integrating children with special needs into mainstream schools has necessitated closer liaison and co-operation between the services and the sectors.

Portage schemes

These are run by health authorities and are used in collaboration with parents in the home and with adults in other under-fives settings. The scheme provides support for parents with children who are handicapped or have other special educational needs. Portage provides a structured programme of learning tailored to the individual needs of the child. Basic skills and concepts are broken down into small steps to give parents and Portage workers a clear idea of which areas to prioritize. Portage workers may also visit children in school to provide continuity for the child and support for the teacher. Parents are regarded as essential partners in the educational process and the programme is based on the shared expertise of parents and professionals.

Voluntary sector

Playgroups

The playgroup movement began during the 1960s as a self-help initiative in response to the lack of provision for the under-fives. Originally it was seen as a preserve of the articulate middle classes but over the years it has become more broadly based. Numbers are still highest where there is little maintained provision.

Playgroups are funded by a combination of fees, grants and fund raising. They are run by volunteers who may have a background in teaching or care. Around 80 per cent of playgroups are affiliated to the Pre-School Playgroups Association (PPA), a registered educational charity. Other playgroups are run privately by individuals and by local authorities. Training courses are offered by the PPA and in some areas training is a requirement for the registration of a group. The number of places provided in 1990 was 407,000.

Provision is part-time, usually for a set number of sessions per week, according to demand and the availability of places.

Fees are charged and some local-authority subsidies are available, depending on need. The Rumbold Report noted that around 700 PPA-affiliated groups offered extended hours, whilst 200 were opportunity groups catering for children with special educational needs. A further 25,000 children with special needs were integrated into other playgroups (DES, 1990, p. 3).

Playgroups have certain advantages. They offer relatively low-cost provision, are responsive to local needs and help to involve parents in children's education outside the home. However, the quality of provision is variable in terms of the environment, facilities, resources and the educational content. Playgroups are housed in a wide variety of places – church halls, scout huts, community centres, private houses, spare classrooms in primary schools. Not all offer the best or even an appropriate environment for young children. Some are without access to outdoor space, and lack the funds to invest in large climbing equipment and mobile toys.

Their educational content and effectiveness have also been questioned (ESAC, 1988, p. xxxvii). This report considered that playgroups would benefit from closer liaison with schools and input from the educational advisory service. Another problem is the low rates of pay and high staff turnover, particularly as women have been attracted back into the workforce. Also, the fees charged, however small, can prove an obstacle for parents on low incomes. Given that they cater for large numbers of children and are often the only form of provision available, the playgroup movement warrants further support and direction.

Parent/toddler groups

These are provided by a range of organizations such as the PPA, church and other charitable groups. Like playgroups, they are run by volunteers on a self-help basis. Hours vary, but generally parents and carers meet for a couple of hours but still have responsibility for their children whilst they play.

Private sector

Childminders

Childminders are permitted to care for children in their own homes. They offer flexible care according to the arrangements made between the childminder and the parent. The ratios are children under 5, 1 to 3; children between 5 and 7, 1 to 6; children aged under 8, of whom no more than three are under 5, 1 to 6.

Childminding grew out of the tradition of local people meeting local needs. More recently, numbers have expanded considerably to meet the needs of working parents so that it is now the largest childcare service for the under-fives. Ferri has argued that its continued popularity is based on the notion that 'it is in tune with the dominant ideological perspective which . . . emphasises *parental* responsibility and power in respect of childcare arrangements made for children' (1992, p. 5).

Childminders have their own professional organization – the National Childminding Association. This was formed in 1977, originally as a self-help and support group. It is now a pressure group in its own right and, as well as offering advice and information to members, has taken on an important role with local-authority departments in terms of co-operation and co-ordination.

Childminding provides the flexibility needed by working parents and offers home-based rather than institutionalized care within small family groups. Children may still attend other forms of pre-school provision. No qualifications are needed, which has helped to perpetuate the low status of childminders, although training has been available in some authorities for a number of years. It is seen as a natural extension of the mothering role rather than as skilled and demanding work.

Under the requirements of the Children Act, childminders have to be registered with the local authority and inspected to ensure that provision complies with certain standards in terms of safety, environment, facilities and the quality of education offered. Local authorities are empowered to provide a range of advisory and support services as well as courses in training and counselling. Training for childminding is also included in the National Vocational Qualifications. Over the coming years, this may help to raise the status of childminders and improve the quality of the service they offer.

Nannies

Nannies provide care for children in their own homes, again according to the individual needs of the family. Many are trained nursery nurses, but training is not compulsory. Children may also be looked after by au pairs who combine household duties with childcare. Concern has been expressed about the use of untrained au pairs from other countries who are significantly cheaper but may not provide an adequate level of care or education.

Private nurseries

These include independent schools, private day nurseries and workplace nurseries. They differ in the extent and form of provision offered according to the age range catered for and the different emphases on care and education. Generally, a ratio of one adult to eight children applies. If individual settings claim to have a distinctive educational emphasis, there should be a qualified teacher and a nursery nurse with a minimum ratio of two to twenty-six.

Independent and pre-prep schools usually cater for 2- to 5-year-olds during school hours and have a distinctive educational emphasis. Private day nurseries and workplace nurseries cater for 0- to 5-year-olds and offer full- or part-time care. Some allow parents to visit during the day for feeding and continuity of contact, particularly with young babies. All are fee-paying, profit-making organizations.

Workplace nurseries may be subsidized by employers' contributions. The availability of such provision is concentrated more in white-collar and professional occupations, particularly where employers value retaining trained personnel rather than continually recruiting and retraining.

The training and backgrounds of staff in these nurseries may vary widely from untrained to nursery nurses and teachers. Premises, resources and the educational quality of private provision is variable. Under the terms of the Children Act, all have to be inspected and registered. Private day-care provision caters for about 2 per cent of under-fives – double that in the public sector. It was the fastest-growing sector in the 1990s.

In addition to the main forms of provision outlined above, there are a number of other services for the under-fives such as One O' Clock Clubs and Play Centres run by local-authority leisure departments. Some authorities also fund a Playbus scheme, particularly in rural areas where there is little or no provision. These provide mobile play facilities and the opportunity for parents to meet.

Toy libraries are run by schools, social services, health authorities and voluntary groups and may be affiliated to the National Toy Libraries Association. They provide a low-cost loan service to the local community and are staffed by volunteers. Parents can also obtain informal advice about child development, play and suitable toys.

The Kids Club Network organizes after-school and holiday activities, again on a voluntary basis. In all cases, adults may come from different training backgrounds – nursery nurses, play leaders, community workers or untrained volunteers.

Quality and inequality

This outline has described the wide range of provision which exists for the under-fives. It has revealed significant variations in the quantity of provision available for different social groups and in different areas of the country. In addition, there are fundamental distinctions between the forms of provision which can affect the quality of care and education which young children receive. These will now be examined in further detail.

In terms of quantity, provision varies widely within and between authorities. There tends to be a higher concentration of publicly funded provision in urban areas, particularly those with a history of Labour-controlled local government. Provision in rural areas is even more ad hoc, relying on local initiatives and self-help groups.

It is not just the issue of quantity, but also of access which is problematic. Even where choices exist, it cannot always be taken for granted that provision meets the needs of children and their families. A study by Osborn and Milbank (1987) found significant inequalities related to social class and ethnicity in access to pre-school provision. Out of a cohort of children born in 1970, 46 per cent of the most disadvantaged children had received no form of pre-school education as compared with 10 per cent of the most advantaged. Similar inequalities existed for children from ethnic minority groups. Forty-six per cent of Indian and Pakistani children and 35 per cent of Afro-Caribbean children had no pre-school experience, compared with 28 per cent of white European children.

These figures raise some important questions. If children from ethnic minority groups are being denied access to provision, this may indicate racist attitudes. It is widely acknowledged that black people are under-represented in the field of early years care and education and that provision and services can be racist (Siraj-Blatchford, 1992, p. 110). It may be that local services are not sufficiently well publicized in local community languages. Or, equally problematic, provision may not meet the needs of families if their languages are not spoken; if their culture and lifestyles are not represented in the curriculum; or if their beliefs and values are not understood or respected. This has clear implications for the recruitment and training of workers in this field, and for the curriculum content of the different types of provision.

Families in low-income groups may be dependent on free or subsidized publicly funded provision. If this is in short supply the cost of alternatives may limit or deny choice. At one nursery school in the south-west of England, each new intake brought around three times as many applicants as there were places. It was the only maintained provision in an area of high unemployment and social deprivation. The headteacher dreaded the admissions meeting with social workers and health visitors where places had to be allocated on the basis of defined need and risk, knowing that there were so many children who would benefit from a place.

The issue of equality is also relevant to children with special educational needs. The Warnock Report (1978) was the first to consider provision for pre-school children in this category and emphasized this as a priority for attention. Where possible, integration into existing forms of provision was recommended, but special schools were to be kept for those children whose needs could not be met adequately elsewhere. For the under-fives, the general shortage of provision, particularly with appropriate facilities and professional skills, has meant that not all children with special educational needs are getting the quality of experience and support that they require and deserve. This is in spite of the positive benefits of early identification, intervention and remediation across a range of needs and disabilities. With tight budgets, local authorities and schools may tailor the support offered to what they can afford rather than to the needs of the child. Penn and Riley (1992) have argued this point forcibly:

> If policies exist which cannot be implemented because of the unevenness and shortage of resources, then the injustices have to be articulated and the strains of the system made clear. (p. 59)

It is a matter of considerable concern that certain groups of children may be further disadvantaged by insufficient, inadequate or inappropriate provision. The issue of quality is of increasing significance in view of the number of research studies which indicate that good-quality provision can enhance development and create a positive cycle of performance and expectations. Poor-quality provision, on the other hand, does not. Any discussion about quantity and quality must also address notions of equity and equality, access and accessibility.

It is not just the quantity of provision that is variable. The quality between the different settings for under-fives differs widely in many respects. This reflects many complex interacting factors. Adults working in this field often do their very best within limited means and resources and the fact that all provision does not meet certain standards, particularly in terms of children's education, is not necessarily directly attributable to them. Often it reflects historical influence and precedent, the failure of policy at local and national levels, inadequate funding, insufficient training and career progression and the low status of under-fives workers. Nevertheless, the pre-school experience of many under-fives is simply not good enough. Some of the reasons for this will now be explored.

First, the backgrounds and training of adults are diverse. As shown above, some settings do not require any formal training whilst others have clearly defined criteria. Degrees are mandatory for all teachers and are required for some levels of social work. Nursery nurses undergo a two-year training course which enables them to work with 0- to 8-year-olds. There are other courses at different levels in social work, care, health, play, childminding and playgroups. Each of these has had its own validating body with different standards and requirements so that progression between levels has, in the past, been difficult. Recent changes in outlook, moves towards inter-disciplinary and multi-professional training and the introduction of National Vocational Qualifications (NVQs) have begun to address some of the problems inherent in this field. The Rumbold Report (DES, 1990) recommended a pattern of training and qualifications for childcare workers which would bridge the gap between vocational and academic qualifications. The Children Act (1989) also stresses the importance of improving training, progression and career structures, and recognizing the complexity of working with the under-fives.

However, it has been the case that different training backgrounds have produced workers with widely varying perceptions of their role, children's needs, the aims and purposes of the setting in which they work and their priorities. This is further complicated by personal beliefs and values which exert a strong influence on practice. This can cause difficulties within different settings and between the sector providers and presents a challenge in terms of better communication and co-ordination.

A further problem is that of the status of all adults who work with the under-fives. Even within the teaching profession, nursery teachers are seen as having less pressure and an easier job with children playing all day rather than engaging in real education. The abilities of young children and the demands upon teachers have been seriously underestimated. Nursery teachers have also found it more difficult to secure career progression and to undertake further professional studies which are geared towards the under-fives. The ESAC report (1988), the Rumbold Report (DES, 1991) and the HMI report on the under-fives (DES, 1989) all noted these factors and recommended appropriate pre- and in-service training and the need for a stronger emphasis on the value and status of nursery teachers.

Similar attitudes are common throughout the education and caring professions. Historically, work with the under-fives has been seen as exclusively the domain of women – a natural extension of their role as primary care givers. It has often proved convenient for women to fit their jobs around the demands of their families. But for the vast majority, the work is low paid and certainly does not attract the recognition it deserves in terms of the inherent challenges and demands.

The environments in which children and adults work also vary significantly. Where provision is purpose built, the needs of children are taken into account in terms of space, facilities, access, safety and the range of activities. Even in the maintained sector, ideal conditions are not always guaranteed, particularly where nursery classes have been slotted in to surplus space in primary schools. As noted above, playgroups and parent/toddler groups spring up in all sorts of places. Under the Children Act, local authorities have a duty to inspect all forms of provision and it may be that groups will be closed because of inadequate facilities and failure to comply with standards. This raises concerns about quantity versus quality when really both are needed.

Resources are another issue in the debate about quality. At national and local government level, those in Health, Education and Social Services have to prioritize between competing demands for funds. Successive years of cutbacks in public sector finance have done little to enhance the status of the under-fives. We have already seen how the educational reforms from 1988 onwards have taken precedence over investment in nursery education. In one primary school, the nursery capitation was withheld for two years on the basis that new reading and maths schemes were needed for the older children. Some voluntary groups, particularly those reliant on charitable donations, struggle from year to year just to keep going. Educational toys, games, books and other resources are major items of expenditure, not always affordable by the voluntary groups.

Finally, the curriculum offered to children in different settings varies considerably and can directly influence the quality of educational experience and the child's later performance in school. This applies as much to the under-threes as it does to children aged from 3 to 5. Much more is understood now about how young children learn and develop. Consequently, knowledge about what constitutes an appropriate curriculum for this age group is extensive. These issues will be explored in greater depth in Chapters 5 and 6, but it is important to note that recent thinking in this field has moved towards the notion of care and education as being inseparable. In the past it has been a false assumption that some children need one and not the other. Good-quality care is educational, just as good-quality education is caring. Both are fundamental to a high-quality curriculum for the under-fives.

As we come towards the end of the twentieth century, it is useful to identify the trends and features which are discernible from the legacy of the last hundred years. The under-fives are still regarded as a low priority, vulnerable to cutbacks in times of recession but not sufficiently important to warrant large-scale investment in times of prosperity. There still exists a culture of self-help, charitable support and 'making do'. For many families, provision might not be as good as it could or should be, but often it is better than nothing.

The notions of rescue, protection and compensation are still evident in the public-sector services. Indeed this seems to have reinforced the three-tier system which has always operated: those who can afford private-sector provision, those who continue to use different forms of free or low-cost provision according to local supply, and those who are channelled into publicly funded provision on the basis of identified need. Moss and Melhuish have argued that the clear objective of government policy

> is to encourage and provide a private market in under-fives services, paid for by parents (sometimes with the support of employers) and only diluted by a limited amount of State nursery education and very small quantities of public day care for children 'in need'. The Government want to see the market provide diversity, choice and good quality. Issues of access, equality and segregation receive no attention. (1991, p. 84)

It can be argued that this policy reflects economic and social differences within society. It also reinforces divisiveness and inequity from the earliest years of life.

We have seen how a range of factors have a direct bearing on the quality of educational experience for the under-fives. We know that current levels of provision do not meet the needs of working parents, nor do they meet parents' demands for high-quality education, particularly in the maintained nursery sector. We also know that provision does not meet children's needs in the best possible ways. Clearly much progress is needed at all levels to address some of the problems inherent in this field. This has implications for policy makers, parents and practitioners, particularly if a culture of partnership and co-operation is to thrive. The next chapter will examine policy developments and social trends in recent years in order to set out a framework for progress towards the twenty-first century.

Chapter 3
CHANGE AND CHALLENGE

In this chapter I will outline recent legislative, educational and political changes and examine their impact on the under-fives. The challenges to policy makers at local and national level will be related to social and economic trends and changes in the patterns of family life.

The Children Act 1989

The Children Act has major implications for all those involved with the under-fives, at all levels. The recommendations cut across traditional boundaries, establish rights and responsibilities and demand new ways of working with and on behalf of children. The Act's emphasis on family support and partnership with parents requires local authorities to adopt new approaches to childcare services, and new priorities in terms of resource allocation. The overall philosophy is one of protection from harm, abuse and neglect and promotion of rights and responsibilities. For children in need, the Act considers that the best place for a child to be brought up is usually within the family and that the local authority, working in partnership with parents, should endeavour to provide the range and level of services appropriate to the child's needs.

The implications of the Act for services and provision for the under-fives are extensive. However, whilst it offers the possibility of considerable progress, it also creates some difficult problems. The Act specifies standards in day-care services and lays down requirements for registration and inspection. Day-care providers for 0- to 8-year-olds must be registered with the Social Services Department for the following reasons.

* to protect the child;

- to provide suitable premises and a safe environment while the child is being cared for away from home;
- to ensure good quality care is provided and maintained;
- to ensure that the providers have relevant qualifications, training and experience in looking after children;
- to provide assurance to the parent that their child is being well looked after in a safe and supportive environment;
- to encourage activities which are appropriate to the child's age and development;
- to ensure good quality play provision.

The Act also gives a comprehensive definition of a 'fit person' to work with young children. The local authority should have regard to the following points:

- previous experience of looking after or working with children;
- qualifications and/or training in a relevant field;
- the ability to provide warm and consistent care;
- knowledge of equal opportunities;
- commitment and knowledge to treat all children as individuals and with equal concern;
- physical health;
- mental stability, integrity and flexibility;
- known involvement in criminal cases involving abuse to children and other relevant cases.

The local authority also has to be satisfied that other people living or working on the premises with substantial access to children are fit to be in the proximity of children under 8.

Details of adult/child ratios and appropriate qualifications have already been given in Chapter 2. Settings which provide full-time group care should have a range of support staff including cooks, cleaners and clerical staff, so that those employed to provide care and education for the children are not required to prepare food, carry out other domestic tasks, routine administration, or be involved in maintenance of the premises or equipment. This should have the effect of releasing staff from daily chores and allowing them to spend more time interacting with the children.

There are further detailed requirements regarding space, access, minimum safety standards, hygiene and welfare. The Act stipulates that corporal punishment should not be used, including smacking, slapping and shaking. Day-care staff and other providers should not be judgemental or critical of parents, and should have regard for the family's religious persuasion, racial origin, cultural and linguistic background:

> All young children are growing up in a multicultural society where differences should be welcomed and encouraged. Critical, judgemental approaches only serve to damage children.

The Act places a 'clear, positive and separate' duty on local authorities to provide services for children with disabilities and special educational needs. A child is considered to be in need if

(a) he is unlikely to achieve or maintain, or to have the opportunity for achieving or maintaining, a reasonable standard of health or development without the provision for him of services by a local authority;

(b) his health or development is likely to be significantly impaired, or further impaired, without the provision for him of such services;

(c) he is disabled.

The child's needs are taken to include physical, emotional and educational needs according to age, sex, race, religion, culture, language and the capacity of carers to meet those needs.

Local authorities are required to keep a register of children with disabilities and to ensure that their needs are met. This is intended to facilitate planning of the right level and mix of services to meet their existing and future needs as adults. The emphasis is on developing services for children and their families, and to give support to families in their own homes and in the local community. This has implications for funding, co-operation, consultation and co-ordination between the different service providers, voluntary organizations and parents.

In the past, parents who have children with special needs have not always had access to the full range of services required. Reasons for this have included poor co-ordination within and between services, a shortage of trained personnel, insufficient services to meet demands and a lack of information to parents as to what services were available and how they could be accessed.

As well as inspection and registration, local authorities now have a duty to review services for the under-fives every three years. Information from the review is intended to provide a 'feed-forward' system for all service providers on future development and policy implications. The first review was carried out jointly between education and social services in autumn 1992. Because of the wide-ranging scope of the Act, authorities have had to draw up extensive criteria, some quantitative and some qualitative. Quantitative data is relatively easily obtained – the range of services, numbers attending, compliance with the service standards on ratios, health and safety. However, qualitative information is much more problematic, for this relates to the extent to which the different types of provision are meeting the child's needs, whether they are adopting the criteria for equal opportunities, and whether they are of sufficiently high quality in terms of educational content.

Assessing quantitative features is a straightforward task – virtually a tick sheet on a clipboard exercise. However, evaluating the quality of provision is more complex since it involves value judgements as to what are essential quality criteria. In each authority, the reviews are carried out in relation to policies on day care and early years education, children in need, services for children with special educational needs, equal opportunities including race, gender, disability and how these are developed and monitored. This has created a number of problems.

First, local authorities have had to work out their own policy frameworks for all these areas. Some already had clearly defined policies for the under-fives, with co-ordinators, working groups, monitoring procedures and quality criteria for policy and practice. Some were less well organized and were having to forge links and develop appropriate policies and strategies (Penn and Riley, 1992, Chapter 5). The difficulties encountered have been formidable and have exposed the problems of working towards the requirements of the Children Act not just across various departmental boundaries, but within different political ideologies and priorities at local government level. And all are subject to cutbacks in public-sector spending imposed by central government.

Second, the different service providers all have their own concepts and definitions of quality. Even if quality could be defined how could it be guaranteed that quality criteria could be met in all the different settings to an adequate level? The outline of provision given in Chapter 2 indicated the extent to which settings differ in terms of environment, resources, priorities and children's educational experiences. Even within maintained nursery schools and classes there can be significant variations in the quality of the curriculum offered (Smith, 1992). The quality criteria laid down by HMI (DES, 1989) and the Rumbold Report (DES, 1990) are difficult to achieve since they demand a high level of skill, expertise and knowledge on the part of adults who work with young children. This again raises the question about training, resourcing and status.

The danger is that the review process will concentrate on those surface features which are more easily quantifiable, and neglect issues relating to quality. Ideally, the registration officers and review team should have specialized knowledge about all aspects of the curriculum for the under-fives in order to make any qualitative judgements. The Children Act represents significant progress in the ways in which we should regard and treat children in society. It also gives support and direction to anti-racist education and anti-discriminatory practices.

However, the Act only lays down minimum standards. It does not require any expansion to meet overall demands for pre-school education, although it may result in improved services and provision for children in need. It places a duty on the public purse to inspect and review all forms of private provision to ensure standards and promote accountability. It is less clear if and how quality will be developed. It is still at the mercy of political will and finance to ensure that children and their families receive the maximum benefit from this legislation.

The Education Reform Act

Children under 5 have also been influenced by the educational reforms of the 1980s. The 1988 Education Reform Act (ERA) was based on the belief of the Conservative government that state education was failing to produce sufficiently high standards, particularly in literacy and numeracy. Blame for this was laid variously at the door of trendy left-wing teacher trainers, the prevalence of so-called progressive methods and, in the early years, too much play and not enough formal instruction.

This Act had a direct bearing on the under-fives in several different respects. It instituted the National Curriculum for 5- to 16-year-olds with three core subjects – English, Maths and Science – and seven foundation subjects – technology, history, geography, music, art, physical education, dance and drama. Religious education was treated separately. Tests were introduced for children at the end of the key stage – 7, 11 and 14. These reforms raised some important questions about the under-fives.

First, because of the widely different pre-school experiences of children, were they effectively unequal by 5? High-quality nursery provision was perceived increasingly as giving children a 'head start' into Key Stage 1 so that some could be seen as disadvantaged either by lack of maintained provision, or by the low educational quality of what was available. The varied entry policies adopted by local authorities meant that children were experiencing different periods of schooling before 7, according to where they lived and the policies of schools in the local area. Again, was early entry to school creating further advantage by giving children a longer period of school before testing at 7?

The introduction of a 'subject-based' curriculum gave rise

to considerable debate about what was an appropriate curriculum for this age group. The pronouncements being made by the Conservative government were at odds with the recommendations of the ESAC report (1988), the HMI report (1989) and the Rumbold Report (1990). The 'back to basics' cry seemed to devalue what had been widely regarded as good practice in the early years – integrated approaches to planning, discovery learning, first-hand experience and play.

The relationship of the National Curriculum to the under-fives curriculum was equally unclear. If nursery teachers had certain reservations, the situation was also problematic from the perspective of other under-fives workers outside education who had little or no access to the National Curriculum documents, and little involvement in the debate or awareness of these issues. The idea of a national curriculum for the under-fives was mooted but was not adopted on the grounds of desirability or feasibility. Given the wide variety of settings, it would have been impossible to implement. The introduction of testing children at 5 was still being considered by the Secretary of State for Education, John Patten, in 1993. The purpose of this was to gain a better measure of progress between 5 and 7, but testing at 5 might also have the effect of teasing out differences between children based on their pre-school experiences. Teachers of reception-age children tend to carry out their own baseline assessment of children on entry to primary school, but do not administer standardized, formal tests which would yield comparable data across all 5-year-olds.

At the same time that the government was introducing these reforms, several research reports were critical of some aspects of nursery education in the maintained sector, raising questions about the content, quality and effectiveness of provision. These reports, and the sometimes heated debate about the National Curriculum, all served to foreground more rigorous discussion of children's pre-school experience and what constitutes an appropriate curriculum for the under-fives.

The Education Reform Act also had the effect of introducing market forces and an enterprise culture into state education.

Originally it was intended that the results of testing at 7, 11 and 14 would be published with schools ranked in league tables in terms of their performance. This was supposed to enable parents to choose the school with the 'best' results, creating an ethos of competition and 'survival of the fittest'. Parents and children were to be regarded as consumers and clients, creating a demand for high-quality provision and services like so many goods in a shopping trolley. Parents were given a stronger voice in the running of schools on governing bodies, and the right to vote on whether schools should opt out of local government control and become grant-maintained.

Under the Local Management of Schools (LMS), each school became responsible for its own budget with a certain amount of discretion as to how that is allocated on a yearly basis. In order to maximize income and make use of space, many schools have developed initiatives which have forged links between the pre-school and statutory phases, again on a local, ad hoc basis. Although public-sector nursery provision is expensive, it has not been replaced as a result of LMS. It has always been popular with parents and a nursery class is of benefit in attracting pupils to a primary school. It remains to be seen whether this will increase demand for more nursery provision and, if so, whether there will be an increasing tendency to charge for it in order to cover costs, particularly if central or local government are unwilling to commit funds in this area. It is also possible that headteachers may be tempted to reduce costs by employing nursery nurses rather than nursery teachers. A further 'enticement' has been early entry to school, again potentially reducing the costs of childcare for parents. Absorbing 4-year-olds into reception classes has also had the effect of altering the nature of nursery provision, where it is available, with a higher proportion of 3-year-olds and less time spent in a nursery before transfer to school.

The introduction of market forces into the public sector has been criticized in many respects, not least because it neglects the fundamental point that every child should have access to high-quality provision, regardless of where they live, their economic status, or how articulate and demanding their parents are. Choice and diversity are not attainable for parents in low-income groups, or in isolated rural areas, without personal transport or the means to afford public transport. With regard to the under-fives, we have also seen that choice and diversity are not realistic ideals where there is so much unevenness in the quantity and quality of provision. This remains an issue not just for pre-school provision, but for 4-year-olds in infant classes as well.

Both the Children Act and the Education Reform Act have introduced a framework for change. However, these two major pieces of legislation for and about children do not work together as closely, or as harmoniously, as they might. It remains to be seen whether consumer demand and parental involvement will have any impact on some of the key issues identified in this book – supply, access, continuity, quality and equality.

In addition to the developments outlined above, there have also been significant changes in health and social services which impact on young children and their families. Both departments have been restructured in terms of management and funding, again with market forces playing a determining part in what is available, and how priorities should be defined. This is likely to have an effect on community services, provision for children with special educational needs and support services for families with young children. Although children are, theoretically at least, entitled to the range of provision and services outlined in Chapter 2, it is not always guaranteed that they will receive some or all of what they actually need, particularly if other priorities continue to take precedence over the under-fives as they have done in the past. Again, market forces and the enterprize culture seem to be creating further divisiveness, between those who can afford to pay, those within reach of good services, and those who have to make do with the minimum available. Both departments are faced with meeting growing demands in the face of diminishing resources. In order to appreciate the task faced in terms of developing well co-ordinated structures, and reconiling resources with growing demands, it is necessary to understand the context of social change in Britain in the late twentieth century.

Children and their families

The notion that children under 5 are better off at home and that the mother is the primary caregiver has been challenged by changes in family life and employment. These have been influenced by a range of factors: the needs of employers and the labour market; the feminist movement which has supported women's rights to work and has challenged prevailing values and attitudes towards women in society; and shifting trends in family size and structure. All have had an impact on the lives of young children and those who work with them.

In terms of employment, women form an increasingly large proportion of the civilian labour force. The number of women in the workforce has grown by around one million since the mid 1980s and is expected to continue growing into the twenty-first century so that women will make up 50 per cent of the labour force. 'In the workforce' includes women who are employed as well as those who are unemployed and claiming benefit. In 1991, over half of all women of working age were economically active.

These changes have come about because of the increase in part-time jobs, a decrease in the number of school leavers, lower birth rates, small families and the higher average age at which women have children. Women in the professional, employer and manager classes are more likely to be economically active than women from other groups. Two-thirds of women in this group who have a very young child are in employment. For all socio-economic groups, women are most likely to be in full-time work if they have no dependent children. Statistics show that the number of mothers working full-time is lowest where the child is between 0 and 4 years old. The number of mothers working full- and part-time increases as children get older.

What implications do these statistics have for the under-fives? Women in the professional, employer and manager

45

classes are more likely to be able to afford childcare, or to receive subsidies from employers in the form of childcare vouchers or a workplace nursery. In economically stringent times, employers have become more aware of the need to retain employees rather than incur recruitment and training costs. However, for those who receive no subsidies, childcare is an expensive undertaking. For example, one professional couple spent £400 per month for their 4-year-old, which included a childminder and part-time attendance at a private nursery – there was no public provision available. Clearly such costs can be prohibitive to those on lower incomes. In 1993 a young mother was jailed for leaving her 2-year-old at home whilst she went out to work. For her, the choice was between paying for food and rent or a childminder. Whatever the rights and wrongs of the case, it does highlight the dilemmas which parents may face, particularly if they are lone parents.

The percentage of all families with dependent children that are lone-parent families has more than doubled since 1971, from 8 per cent to 18 per cent in 1991. Only a small proportion of lone parents are fathers. This reflects the rise in both divorce and the number of births outside marriage. The number of marriages is falling, whilst the number of divorces is rising. Divorce has increased for couples at every age, but rates are highest in the 25 to 29 age group where it is likely that young children will be involved.

In the 1990s, lone parents were stigmatized as social security scroungers by the New Right of the Conservative Party on the assumption that they had all chosen that status in order to avail themselves of state benefits. This ignored some basic facts. Many lone parents have experienced bereavement or desertion. Others have chosen separation as a way out of violent, abusive, damaging or unhappy relationships which had a negative impact on them and their children. Children of lone parents are also sometimes stigmatized as coming from unstable and impoverished backgrounds. Again, such views conceal a more objective appraisal. What seems to be important for all children is the basic stability of the family unit, whether with one or two parents.

Bringing up children is a demanding task, particularly as a lone parent. It is not necessarily the fact of being a lone parent but other associated problems which can give rise to difficulties. For those in higher income brackets, the stresses and tensions do not appear to be as great. Those on lower incomes inevitably have a low standard of living, particularly if they are in poor or overcrowded housing or in bed and breakfast accommodation. The number of homeless families with children rose by 46 per cent during the 1980s and three-quarters of children from lone-parent families live in poverty, that is below the weekly average wage. At the same time, improvements in living standards, health and welfare actually reversed for poorer families, with increased child poverty and greater inequalities between the richest and poorest members of society. The lack of provision for young children is often exacerbated by the lack of play areas in both rural and urban areas, as well as considerations of safety. Single parents may feel the additional stress and frustration of having few choices and little power in their lives. For many families, the lack of childcare support serves to reinforce the poverty trap and prevents people from entering employment, further or higher education.

For working parents, the stresses and tensions can be differently problematic. Where one or both parents choose to or have to work, leaving a child in the care of another person can be a traumatic experience as the following examples show. One mother was due to return to work when her first child was six months old. She had an employer-subsidized place at a nursery in the centre of London and was spending a week with her son at the nursery to get to know the staff and routines. Although she was happy with the quality of the nursery, she was increasingly distressed about separation from her child and her ability to cope with a demanding job. Her preferred solution would have been longer maternity leave, a job share or childcare vouchers for a local childminder. None of these options was available.

Another mother with children in the same nursery left home with them at 6.30 every morning for a one and a half

hour drive into London. They were in the nursery from 8 a.m.
to around 5 p.m., with a long return journey at the end of
every day. This mother said that there was only time to feed
and bath the children before putting them to bed, and that
was often fraught because they were all tired. She knew they
were getting very little 'quality time' together and felt that
her own priorities had changed in terms of her career and her
role as a mother. However, a career break was not an option
and the nature of her work ruled out a job share. The staff
in the nursery were aware of the anxieties of many of their
parents and the effects on the children of lengthy separation.
They were concerned about whether the children were becoming institutionalized at a young age despite their best efforts
at replicating everyday homely activities as part of a broad
and stimulating curriculum.

There is no escaping the fact that the current levels, range
and quality of pre-school provision are not always in the best
interests of the under-fives or their families. As noted at the
start of this book, children are the least powerful members of
society. They do not vote, they do not have a powerful voice
and cannot form pressure groups to promote their interests.
They are reliant upon adults to define, implement, uphold
and defend their rights. This begs the question of whether
we, as adults, give sufficient thought to the needs of young
children who inherit a future we create for them. Current
levels of provision and the fragmented nature of services for
the under-fives reflect the low status of children in our society,
and of the adults who work with them. Without a clear consensus between parents, employers and politicians, children
will remain vulnerable and undervalued.

Images of childhood

As Pugh has stated (1992, p.1), how we perceive children and
childhood is a reflection of the values of the society in which
we live. Attitudes towards children have changed markedly
over the centuries in accordance with the wealth and con-
dition of society as a whole. In the twentieth century, we
regard childhood as a period in its own right, not just as a

preparation for adulthood. So how does this influence children's lives? David (1993a, Chapter 2) has argued that in this country children are seen as the property of their parents. It is still regarded as acceptable for parents to smack, slap and hit their children (domestic corporal punishment) even though it is a criminal act if adults hit each other as a means of enforcing discipline or exerting moral control. Statistics show that the under-fives are most at risk from physical, sexual and emotional abuse. This occurs across all socio-economic groups and is most often perpetrated by parents and family members, including older children. It is all too easy to become over-sentimental about young children and ignore the fact that many live fractured, unhappy lives. Homelessness, poverty, family stress, dislocation and abuse all impinge upon the health, welfare and development of children. Both provision and services for the under-fives and their families have failed to keep pace with social and economic changes so that the 'rising tide of social need' identified by Van der Eyken in 1969 is still rising a quarter of a century later.

Although children are no longer exploited economically by being forced to work from an early age, we need to consider whether they are increasingly exploited psychologically in modern, consumer-oriented societies. As consumers of services, children demand a high level of investment with no promise of an immediate return. As consumers of goods, however, they represent a lucrative market. Over £150 million a year is spent on advertising targeted exclusively at children. Their basic needs for food, warmth, love, shelter and stimulation have spawned an entire designer industry, from clothes, food and toys to furniture, wallpaper and crockery. For some parents, children themselves became the essential designer accessory in the 1980s, a means by which they could express their own status, income and lifestyle. Pressures to early acquisitiveness were acute in the 1980s and 1990s with a constant succession of essential collectables and spin-offs from films and television programmes. Creating want serves the demands of a consumer-oriented society whilst at the same time reinforcing the gap between the rich and poor. Parents can be put under considerable pressure to provide increasingly expensive and sophisticated toys which are soon discarded as the next craze floods the market.

Decisions about lifestyles, parenting and priorities are very much a private matter within individual families except where the state needs to intervene on the grounds of promotion of a child's welfare or protection from harm. However, it can be difficult to balance the needs and interests of children with those of parents, the demands of the economy and pressures within society. These factors create conflicting demands which take concern for the care and education of the under-fives out of the privacy of the family and into the public domain. The needs of children, parents, employers and the economy cannot be met by the private sector and market forces alone. This will only result in a continuing series of ad hoc, narrowly focused initiatives which target employees who are valued and valuable. It will do nothing to address the needs of children in other socio-economic groups.

However, it is difficult to see how flexible, widely available and accessible forms of high-quality provision might be possible without substantial public-sector funding, tax incentives or subsidies to employers and employees. This would imply a radical shift of ideologies and priorities. It would also require a fundamental change of values in relation to how we view children in society. The following chapter will examine a range of perspectives on developing provision for the under-fives in order to identify current trends and future possibilities.

Chapter 4
PROBLEMS AND POSSIBILITIES

The early 1990s began to witness significant changes in attitudes towards the under-fives. This was influenced by a range of factors including research into the effectiveness of pre-school provision, the Children Act, and the publication in November 1993 of an influential report by the National Commission on Education. In this chapter, I will outline some of these changes and examine their implications for the future. I begin by returning to the Children Act and the reviews of provision for the under-fives.

Under the terms of the Children Act (1989) local authorities and local-education authorities are required to carry out a joint review of provision for children under 8 and their families. The Act specifies the review duty and the review process, but it is at the discretion of the two authorities to decide how to discharge this duty. The first of these reviews was undertaken in 1992 and will be repeated every three years. Potentially, this process should enable local authorities to plan future services in a more co-ordinated way, identifying need and demand for provision, training, curriculum development, equal-opportunities policies and support networks for parents and workers.

The Children Act is progressive in its principles and ambitious in its scope and aspirations. How far these can be realized in practice remains to be seen, particularly given central government spending targets and competing priorities. However, the review process has set in motion a framework for development. Theoretically at least local authorities have the opportunity to begin sorting out the under-fives muddle. But what sort of problems and possibilities does this raise? In order to address this question I will give a brief outline of the review duty and process specified in the Children Act. I will then go on to examine a sample of reviews to give some insights into how local authorities have responded and their recommendations for future developments.

The review duty

The purpose of the review is to enable local authorities to work out the level, pattern and range of day care and related services for young children at local level in consultation with health authorities, voluntary organizations, employers and parents. Nursery and primary education facilities are not included but the two authorities are required to inform themselves about quantity and availability. The review covers all day-care services including local-authority facilities, the independent sector and childminding. Arrangements have to be made for consultation and exchange of information with relevant departments. The views of other interested parties should also be sought including local PPA groups, childminding interests, community groups, lone-parent organizations, ethnic minority groups, the private day-care sector, employers and parents. The purpose of the consultation exercise is to enable organizations and individuals to give their views of the existing pattern of services, the need for changes (if any) and developments and how these are to be instituted. The review should also examine related facilities such as advice, training and counselling to day-care providers, childminders and parents.

The review process

The Act acknowledged that the concept of review involves measurement or assessment. Therefore the review should be undertaken within a framework of agreed aims and objectives for the existing services and provision. Local authorities were required to set such aims and objectives and to agree on how the detailed work of the review was to be carried out. The main stages in the process were specified in the Act – setting the terms of reference, assembling data, analysis, consultation, preparing the report of the review, publication and dissemination of the report and follow up.

The report itself has to be made succinct and accessible to a wide audience, including translation into minority languages where necessary. The purpose of the report is to help increase interest in services for young children among the population as a whole and to encourage debate about local services and how their development can produce benefits. The content of the report has to cover ten key areas:

- basic data on services;
- map of the area with the location of facilities marked;
- policies on day care and early years education, children in need, services for children with special educational needs, policies on equal opportunities, including race, gender, disability and how they are developed and monitored;
- centres of excellence and those with unusual or innovative features;
- known problems – for example mismatch of supply and demand, difficulties in staff recruitment, shortage of childminders or difficulties in the operation of the registration system;
- training opportunities;
- range of other support services for families;
- method of conducting the review with details about members involved and the consultation procedures used;
- numbers of local-authority staff involved in services for under-fives and in what capacity;
- changes in provision and plans for the future and monitoring arrangements.

The review process is intended to become part of a continuous rolling programme of development which encourages good quality services planned and delivered in the light of local wishes and expectations. The report of the review demonstrates how local authorities have responded to the Children Act, what problems and possibilities have been identified and what strategies need to be devised to plan for future developments. In the next section, I will examine a sample of reviews from contrasting local authorities in England. These are not intended to be representative of all authorities, nor to give a broad generalized picture. The information is not presented as a rigorous, systematic research study. The purpose is to gain insights into the contexts and processes of change and to consider the possible impact on educating the under-fives.

Reviewing the reviews

A brief examination of a random sample of thirty review reports indicates that local authorities approached this task in different ways and with varied outcomes. The complexity of this task was onerous, with authorities having to use advanced statistical packages and survey methods for collating and interpreting a vast amount of data. Clearly some were better placed than others to undertake this process. There were variations between authorities in their existing managerial systems and strategies. Some had already adopted unified approaches to the management of services with joint decision-making and responsibilities, common goals and objectives. These included joint working and planning groups drawn from education and social services with structures to promote liaison with other relevant groups. Others had only recently begun this process.

The definition of 'early years' varied between the under-fives and the under-eights. Several authorities had an early-years consultative group or forum and smaller local liaison groups overseen by an early years co-ordinator. Many of the reports included statements of aims, principles and curriculum policies, or indicated that these were currently being developed. Shared principles and a clearly defined curriculum policy for the under-fives are seen as important for raising the quality of educational input across different settings, promoting continuity, and establishing common frameworks for progress and training.

Some of the more detailed policies reflect current theories of how children learn, the key features of an effective curriculum and clear guidelines for achieving quality. There were variations in the age ranges covered by the curriculum policies. For example, the Devon and Cheshire policies target 3-and 4-year-olds. Gloucestershire, which has no maintained nursery education, has a curriculum guidance document for the under-fives in family centres and other pre-school groups as well as a resource pack for running play-schemes on school premises. Manchester and Sheffield also focus on the under-fives and set this phase within a 5 to 16 continuum to emphasize the importance of liaison and continuity.

Overall, the reports indicate a strong commitment to expanding provision and services for the under-fives and their families, but there are differences in ethos as to the best or most appropriate ways of achieving this. For example, Cleveland Council states that the primary function of both the local education authority and the social services department is not to provide a form of care which specifically supports a level of economic activity within families. Childcare arrangements are seen as the responsibility of individuals, according to circumstances. In contrast, Manchester City Council considers that childcare should be offered as of right, that parental choice over the length and type of childcare should be possible, that a range of services should be available and that services should be free of charge. Both Leeds and Bradford City Councils also regard better provision and access as part of a broader equal-opportunities programme for giving parents choices about work and family responsibilities.

Clearly, local authorities need to devise realistic policies for future developments, particularly in view of the scope of the task and the limitations of funding. It may be that they take on the function of retaining a core of maintained provision targeted predominantly at children in need, overseeing developments in the private and voluntary sectors and in training. Trends towards this can be discerned in many of these reports, reflecting the terms of the Children Act regarding children in need. Most of the development plans indicate that authorities will locate new provision and services in areas of significant disadvantage and deprivation. For example, Bradford has developed criteria for targeting resources at children most in need of services. 'Priority One' guarantees a service. 'Priority

Two' leads to a service as and when resources are available and only after the needs of children and families in Priority One have been met. Lancashire County Council also has criteria for admission to day-care provision based on a child's special educational needs as well as a range of social, emotional, economic, health and welfare indicators.

Inevitably the reports have thrown into sharp relief many of the constraints placed on local authorities by central government policies so that commitment cannot easily be translated into action. First and foremost is the issue of funding. The Children Act places a responsibility on local authorities to increase their levels of provision, particularly for children in need and at risk. However, many are struggling to maintain their existing levels let alone embark on any significant expansion. Local government spending has been restricted by rate capping and the use of a standard spending assessment formula which does not take account of levels of poverty, unemployment and deprivation within and between authorities. The pace and complexity of legislative change in health, education and social services have also been difficult to monitor and incorporate, particularly where they make competing and conflicting demands.

It is evident from these reports that local authorities will not be able to implement all of their development plans without a significant increase in funding from central government as well as seeking alternative sources of funding. Meaningful, long-term planning is dependent on secure, long-term funding. Short-term initiatives based on one-off grants or charitable donations do little to assist the processes of expansion, integration and co-ordination which are fundamental to future developments.

The scale of the necessary developments can be seen from the action plans and future proposals which each authority has identified as part of the review process. Again, there are common concerns which range over broad and complex areas. In addition to funding, access, quantity, quality and training are identified as major issues.

In terms of quantity and access, the outstanding gaps are

provision which is usable by families on low incomes, by ethnic minority groups and by children with special educational needs. Clearly there is a need for local 'hand-tailored' provision which reconciles demand and supply according to circumstances. Most of the reviews identified the need to obtain more detailed local information in order to facilitate this process and to provide better information to parents and groups.

The issue of quality, as we have seen, is problematic and demands a range of co-ordinated approaches. First, it is necessary to define criteria which are applicable and realizable across all settings, including the private sector. All forms of provision should be publicly accountable. Second, strategies will be required to ensure that these criteria are being met, with appropriate support and training for all under-fives workers. Ultimately they bear the responsibility for developing quality in their practice. Third, resources must be made available to support these processes both in terms of staffing and funding. This is not just a question of changing managerial strategies, it requires a change of culture in central and local government to one which values young children and supports their development as future citizens.

The majority of reports in this limited survey regarded adequate levels of pre- and in-service training for all under-fives workers as a priority, particularly for those working with children who have special educational needs. Many also acknowledged the need to recruit more black people into this sector. The current framework of training is patchy and inadequate. Again this is a complex and expensive area to address involving co-ordination between central and local government and the various training institutions and validating bodies. There is wide recognition of the need for more inter-disciplinary, multi-agency training and for a clearly defined structure which would allow for progression between levels. Such initiatives would eventually help to raise the status of under-fives workers. The task facing local authorities in developing provision for the under-fives is extensive and cannot be addressed without wider support and involvement.

The employers' perspectives

With changes in employment trends and the labour market, the provision of childcare has increasingly become an issue for employers. Many large companies have recognized the value of 'family friendly' policies in enabling them to recruit and retain employees, thus maximizing their competitiveness and commercial potential. Some have responded positively to social and economic changes, introducing equal-opportunities policies, extending maternity leave, allowing for career breaks and flexible working. However, these measures do not solve all the problems faced by parents in employment.

Because the United Kingdom has the second lowest number of childcare places in the European Community, employers have been left to fill the gaps in a number of ways. These include setting up workplace nurseries or providing childcare vouchers to give parents choice and flexibility. Employers have been frustrated by the patchwork of services and the lack of direction and co-ordination by central government. They cannot offer the choice and quality that is needed in every geographical location. The free-market ethos can only work to a limited degree and, as noted earlier, tends to favour those in professional and managerial occupations. Start-up costs for a workplace nursery are considerable, even when shared between a number of companies, and are beyond the reach of smaller businesses. In addition, government tax policies do not provide sufficient incentives either to parents or employers to extend provision substantially. Childcare vouchers are considered a taxable benefit, although a subsidized nursery place is not. As in the past, statements of good intentions about partnership between central and local government, parents and employers have failed to materialize into workable strategies on the required scale.

Again the initiative has been left to employers, resulting in more ad hoc, local solutions, some of which have been threatened by the economic recession. In 1993 a group of large companies formed an organization entitled Employers For Childcare. This was supported by the Confederation of British

Industry and includes the BBC, the Midland Bank, the Trustee Savings Bank, Shell UK and British Gas. The group recognizes that unless there is a nationally recognized childcare policy and strategy, any efforts to enable staff to combine work and family responsibilities can only continue to be piecemeal and fragmentary. Their mission statement acknowledges the need for the government to take the lead in establishing a national policy and enabling genuine partnerships to develop between parents, employers, government, local agencies and providers. The initiative seeks the provision of accessible, available, affordable, quality childcare which meets the differing needs and circumstances of parents and children. This is regarded equally as a business issue as well as a social imperative, particularly in view of the creation of a single European market, the increasing number of women in the workplace and the need to ensure labour mobility.

The political agenda

Any improvements in provision for the under-fives can only be possible with the commitment of influential bodies and individuals with policy and decision-making powers. Early years pressure groups and organizations have been persistent and influential, but ultimately it is political will and funding priorities at central government level which determine large-scale change.

As noted earlier, the 1980s saw many social and economic changes. Several reports which surveyed the impact of these changes also raised awareness of the status of children in society and the inequalities which can be compounded by the lack of adequate provision for the under-fives. The Commission on Social Justice (1993) regarded the level of pre-school provision as one of the fundamental inequities in society and called for universal nursery education, as promised by Margaret Thatcher in 1972.

A report by the Gulbenkian Foundation stated that children are still not adequately protected in our society. Part of the problem was seen as parental and adult attitudes towards children, the lack of co-ordination of services and adequate measures for child protection. This report called for greater acknowledgement of children's rights, including the right to care, to security and a good upbringing, to be heard on any major decision and the right not to be subjected to corporal punishment or any other humiliating or degrading treatment. The number of 'home alone' cases involving young children during Christmas 1993, some involving serious neglect and deprivation, served to highlight the fact that responsibility for upholding children's rights has to be a shared enterprise.

Perhaps the most influential report for some time was that carried out by the National Commission on Education under the chairmanship of Sir Claus Moser. The report, entitled 'Learning to Succeed', was based on an independent inquiry funded for £1 million by the Paul Hamlyn Foundation. It placed the under-fives high on the political agenda, recognizing the potential of early education for all children, and recommended that high-quality, publicly funded nursery education should be available to all 3- and 4-year-olds. As part of wider employment and social policies, good pre-school education and affordable childcare were seen as enabling parents to reconcile the demands of responsible parenting and work outside the home. The report also noted the benefits to the economy and society of better provision for the under-fives – a familiar argument to that put forward by the Fabian Society in 1910.

Such initiatives were seen as part of a long-term programme of development, with local authorities initially targeting provision on children in need. The report endorsed the terms of the Children Act in promoting co-operation between departments, and consultation with service providers and parents, and beginning the process of overcoming fragmented policies and provision. It also acknowledged that it was insufficient only to fund expansion of nursery education. Additional government funding would be needed to enhance the quality of educational experience in other settings, including playgroups, day nurseries and provision for 4-year-olds in school. Improved training and the continuing professional development of all adults who work with the under-fives was regarded

as fundamental to the process of improving quality. The estimated costs of this programme were high, around £860
million, but the Commission stressed that expenditure on a
high-quality education service for the under-fives should be
set against the cost of taking no action:

> We are persuaded that the gains made by children who receive
> high-quality pre-school education will reduce the need for remedial
> education at a later stage, help to ensure that we do not waste
> talent, and perhaps also reduce the social costs which arise from
> youth unemployment and juvenile crime.

By the early 1990s, the case for improved pre-school provision was stronger on social and economic grounds than it
had ever been. Cost-benefit analyses revealed major benefits
to offset the necessary expenditure. As well as the long-term
educational gains noted above, there were also immediate-
term economic gains. These would be accrued by higher
employment among women, and a reduction in families
dependent on welfare benefits. The question shifted from
whether expansion should take place, to where, when and
how quickly. The case for high-quality pre-school provision
and services was no longer in dispute.

Other initiatives also seemed to be leading in a more positive direction. In November 1993, a new allowance for those
on family credit was announced in the budget. This was worth
£28 per week towards the cost of childcare. In December, the
prime minister, John Major, voiced his personal commitment
to wider availability of nursery education at an estimated cost
of £750 million when resources were available. Other options
being considered included parental contribution to the costs
or offering parents childcare vouchers which could be used in
the private sector, thus extending choice and flexibility, at
least in theory.

Whether this was a genuine ideological commitment to the
under-fives or a potential vote winner is a moot point. The
other two main political parties, Labour and the Liberal
Democrats, have had a long-standing commitment to increas-

ing nursery provision. However, as we have seen, this is only part of the solution to a much wider problem.

Pressure for change for the under-fives has been mounting steadily from many different levels in society. The professional associations and trades unions involved with local government, schools, and other pre-school settings have all voiced concerns about the under-fives and related issues. Other early years 'grass-roots' pressure groups and organizations have campaigned consistently in this field, commissioning research, carrying out surveys, organizing conferences, rallies and meetings with policy- and decision-makers. Parents have also played their part, forming self-help and local pressure groups. One group in Exeter campaigned vigorously for additional nursery provision in an area of high unemployment and identified need. The council could not fund this but eventually agreed to set up a family centre.

This chapter has shown that the pressure for change is multi-faceted and multi-layered. The Children Act has set an agenda for future progress which is dependent to a large extent on changes in philosophy, priorities, policies and funding. Another important item on this agenda is changes at the level of practice. The next two chapters will focus on the educational needs of the under-fives and how these can be met in all settings.

Chapter 5

LAYING THE FOUNDATIONS

As we have seen, it is difficult to disentangle the whole question of educating the under-fives from other social, political and economic factors. It is important, therefore, to maintain a clear focus on the needs and interests of children so that these do not become relegated to a position of secondary importance. I begin this chapter by raising the question of why educating the under-fives is an issue in its own right and then go on to consider some of the research and key questions in the debates about the effectiveness of pre-school education. This will lead into consideration of what we mean by the term curriculum and what constitutes an appropriate curriculum for the under-fives.

Early development

Human beings have a long period of growth and development – approximately eighteen years from conception to mature adulthood. The first five years are a period of particularly rapid growth and development, both intellectual and physical. Psychologists have estimated that around 50 per cent of the development of a child's intelligence takes place up to the age of 4, 30 per cent between 4 and 8 and 20 per cent between 8 and 17. From the day they are born, children invest a tremendous amount of energy, will and determination in learning – striving to know and understand their physical and social world and their place within it. Babies may seem at first dependent and helpless but, as Froebel noted, their power of thought is much greater than we imagine.

This rapid phase of growth and development does not mean that a child's intelligence is fixed by the age of 5. Psychologists and educational theorists support the view that learning and development depend on the quality of stimulation during the early years. Current theories indicate that there is a much more complex interaction between heredity, environment and experience than was assumed in the past. It follows, therefore, that attendance at a pre-school setting of whatever type might be expected to have some impact on early learning and development, whether positive or negative. The work of the pioneers – Froebel, Montessori, McMillan and Isaacs – all stressed the positive gains from early education.

The effects of pre-school education

The impact of pre-school education has been studied extensively during the last forty years. The data from both America and Europe have yielded significant results with recommendations for policy and practice. In examining the data, it is important to distinguish between the effects and the effectiveness of pre-school education. Both of these are interrelated, but some studies have focused on the immediate, short-term effects on the child such as cognitive, social and emotional development and behaviour. Others have examined medium-term effectiveness such as the child's later performance in school, and long-term effectiveness such as qualifications, employment and life chances. It is useful to consider these separately as they are informed by different perspectives.

Research into the effects of pre-school education has been concerned more directly with the child, the setting and the family. The debate about effectiveness is a highly political issue, especially in the context of state-funded provision, which is expected to yield some return on the investment. Effectiveness is being measured increasingly by the long-term benefits to the state and society. These two perspectives have raised some important questions about what pre-school education is for and what the benefits are. What needs to be addressed is how these benefits can be ensured for all children across the different forms of provision.

The research background

Because of the wide variety of pre-school provision, it is difficult to get accurate, comparable measures of the effects on young children. As was shown in Chapter 2, there are fundamental differences between the types of provision available in this country. Children may experience a succession of different types of provision, whilst others may have little or no experience of group settings outside the home. Some children use more than one type of provision simultaneously, such as part-time nursery attendance and some playgroup sessions. The age of entry to school varies between 4 and 5 years. Children may also experience different caregivers – parents, relatives, friends, nannies, childminders.

In general, more is known about publicly funded forms of provision because it is usually easier for researchers to gain access to these settings. In the private sector childminding has received considerable attention, but there is less research on private nurseries. We know relatively little about the day-to-day lives of children in their homes, approaches to parenting, lifestyles, attitudes and beliefs, the extent and type of parental involvement and interest in children's experiences in different pre-school settings. All these factors are influential in a child's development and achievements.

It is also interesting to note that some of the studies carried out in the 1970s and 1980s (Clark, 1988) had a different bias according to the type of provision. Research into the effects of day care has been concerned with any possible ill-effects of early separation from the mother and young children being 'institutionalized'. Research into nursery schools and classes has oriented more towards evaluating gains in intellectual performance. Studies in which researchers have carried out tests to measure the effects of pre-school attendance have also tended to focus on assessments in this domain. It is more difficult to assess the affective domain – social, moral and emotional development. In fact, all are important but traditionally we have tended to assign more status to thinking, reasoning and understanding in terms of academic performance rather then social competence. However, the social skills which children acquire in the early years are essential to their success at school and in life.

A broad overview of research into the effects of pre-school education is provided by Clark (1988), Godenir and Crahay (1993) and Hennessy, Martin, Moss and Melhuish (1992). The largest project of this kind to be undertaken in this country was the Child Health and Education Study, based on a sample of just over 13,000 children born in one week in 1970 (Osborn and Milbank, 1987). This study gathered information about the children's pre-school experiences and assessed their progress at age 5 and 10. It concentrated on six types of provision – three in the maintained sector, nursery schools and classes and day nurseries, and three in the private sector, independent nursery schools, playgroups (home-based and hall-based) and independent day nurseries.

Overall, the report concluded that attendance at pre-school settings resulted in improvements in their cognitive ability and educational attainments. There were some statistical differences between the types of provision, but no evidence to suggest that any actually hindered a child's development. Local-authority nursery schools, independent nursery schools and home-based playgroups seemed to produce the most cognitive gains. However, the authors acknowledged the difficulties of having to consider so many intervening variables – the age at which a child starts attending, the frequency of attendance, the number of settings attended and the age of entry to school. There were further differences in the children's home lives and backgrounds – social and economic status, the size and stability of the family unit, type of neighbourhood and ethnic origin.

This report also identified a range of issues which were of wider concern in terms of policy and practice. The research did not seek to identify which type of provision was the best, but to discuss those features which contributed to effectiveness and to examine the implications for all settings. As the report noted, it is difficult to define an optimal learning environment across such a wide variety of settings, let alone achieve it. The success or otherwise of a child's pre-school experience does not rest on one single aspect of the curriculum. The important factors seemed to be the educational role of the adults, the quality of the curriculum offered and the extent of parental involvement and interest. The positive results for children in home-based playgroups indicated that there was potential for childminders to perform a more overtly educational role.

The findings also suggested that children from disadvantaged homes were more likely to gain from pre-school provision than their more advantaged peers. Similar findings were reported by Hennessy *et al.* (1992) in their review of research into children and day care. But, as shown in Chapter 2, participation rates across different socio-economic groups are uneven. This implies that groups of children and their families with the greatest need for extra support are least likely to find it, emphasizing the need for provision which is affordable, accessible and beneficial across all socio-economic groups.

Similar findings about the positive effects of pre-school education have been reported from America. In the 1960s, there was a prevailing view that early deprivation was a major cause of later school failure and that compensatory programmes in the pre-school years would help to break the cycle of disadvantage and underachievement. Under Project Head Start several initiatives were funded by the state, targeted predominantly at the most seriously disadvantaged families, most of whom were Black and Hispanic. This was an expensive project which set high expectations of trying to address the problems of social inequality and poverty. Information from the different initiatives was compiled by the Consortium for Longitudinal Studies, founded in 1975, to provide a comparison of the approaches in order to determine which were ⸱most effective.

Early results seemed to indicate positive effects with some cognitive gains. Fewer children had to be placed in special schools and the number of children who had to repeat a year (retained in grade) was reduced. However, these results began to show that the effects were short-term and that any gains were washed out by the age of 6 or 7. This resulted in reduced funding for the programmes on the basis that pre-school education was not going to fulfil the high expectations set in the 1960s. The potential pitfalls of this feast and famine approach to funding were noted by Osborn and Milbank:

> The saga of the Head Start programme and its evaluation provides a salutary warning of the way in which research findings and public policy interact, so that objectivity in research is constantly in danger of being undermined by pressing political and economic considerations. (1987, p. 19)

However, long-term evaluations of some of the original projects provided further data. Each of the programmes initiated in the 1960s had different approaches, although most included high adult:child ratios, parental involvement and family support. One of these, the Perry Pre-School Project, was based on the work of psychologist Jean Piaget. The curriculum incorporated the plan–do–review process which supported the child's own self-initiated activities. This later became more popularly known as the Highscope curriculum. The long-term evaluations of Highscope have indicated some impressive results in both the short-term effects and long-term effectiveness of this type of curriculum.

In the short term it was reported, as with the other programmes, that children achieved higher scores in IQ tests, in reading and mathematics. It was apparent that this impact on aptitudes and performance was sufficient to change children's and parents' aspirations and attitudes and raise teacher expectations. This was indicated by the long-term results relating to the children's life chances and experiences. Those who had participated in the Highscope programme were found to have lower rates of school failure, higher rates of staying on in further and higher education, higher career aspirations, fewer teenage pregnancies, less drug dependency and lower rates of involvement in crime.

In terms of effectiveness and a return on public investment, the Highscope research has forged strong links. It appears to demonstrate the potential long-term benefits of a high-quality programme for disadvantaged children. Already the results have been influential in this country. In 1993 the Home Office announced a three-year research programme to implement the Highscope curriculum in four inner-city nurseries in Liverpool, Oldham, North Tyneside and Lewisham. The fact that pre-school education has been shown to be cheaper than the costs to society and the economy of juvenile crime and delinquency seems to have been a persuasive factor here.

Longitudinal studies of the effects of pre-school education have been carried out in many European countries (Godenir and Crahay, 1993). Most have indicated similar results to the British and American studies. Of course, the limitations of these results should be acknowledged. It is important not to make broad generalizations based on studies which focused on particular groups of children using different experimental programmes. The fact that pre-school education is being so intensely scrutinized is something of a mixed blessing. On the one hand, it is of considerable values to parents, practitioners and policy-makers to have substantial research evidence to support the value of pre-school education. On the other hand, we need to question the purpose for which these research results are being used since the same findings could conceivably be used to support different policies.

Within the political and economic climate of the 1990s, politicians could argue that an increase in home-based provision is more appropriate to children's needs. This represents a low cost to the state and maintains the ethos of parental responsibility for young children and the costs of childcare. Alternatively, it could be argued by parents and early childhood specialists that all children need and deserve high-quality provision in their own right, in order to increase the benefits and effectiveness, regardless of whether or not their parents work, whether they are at risk or in need or to which socio-economic group they belong. It seems that the immediate benefits to children and their families are being considered of secondary importance to the long-term benefits to society.

Whilst that is an important connection to make, it is a narrow and potentially dangerous justification.

The pre-school sector has always had to justify its existence and prove its worth, particularly publicly funded services and provision. However, it is an unrealistic claim that provision for the under-fives alone can have the effect of reducing social inequality and improving subsequent opportunities and life chances. These are very high expectations for the first five years of a child's life. If the reality falls to match these expectations, there is a danger that a climate of failure will be created, leading to reduced funding for the under-fives. Inequity and inequality of opportunity are problems in society which need to be addressed in many spheres and at many levels. Zigler's comment on the American experience rings true for this country as well:

> The problems of many families will not be solved by early intervention efforts, but only by changes in the basic features of the infrastructure of our society. No amount of counselling, early childhood curricula, or home visits will take the place of jobs that provide decent incomes, affordable housing, health care, optimal family configurations, or integrated neighbourhoods where children encounter positive role models. (1991, p.165)

As noted above, some of the research studies found that early cognitive gains were 'washed out' within a few years of compulsory schooling. The question has to be asked whether this was a failure of pre-school education, or a failure of schools to build upon children's early competences and provide an appropriate curriculum. Clark has argued that

> the more comparable, or at least compatible, the aims at different stages in the educational process the more likely there is to be continued progress, and continuity with extension. It seems unrealistic to expect effects to be maintained over a long period without any reinforcement or without at least some maintenance of an approach. (1988, p. 238)

Clearly, all children need conditions which will enable them to develop, maintain and fulfil their potential. The debate about effects and effectiveness has wider implications beyond the first five years of life and the different settings which children experience.

The research studies also raise some important questions about which particular features of provision are significant in promoting positive effects. These appear to be related to the educative role of the adults, the role of the parents, support for the family and the curriculum offered. Each of these will now be explored in further detail in order to determine their implications for policy and practice. If pre-school education does have positive benefits it is essential that these should be ensured for all children in the different forms of provision.

The educative role of the adults

We have already seen that the type and levels of training required to work with the under-fives varies widely across different settings and that the status of adults in this sector is low. Career structure, progression and opportunities for further training have been limited and limiting. In the social and economic climate of the late-twentieth century this deficit model is no longer acceptable. It is dangerous to perpetuate the myth that working with young children is a natural extension of the mothering role, that it is primarily concerned with caring for children in a benign, protective way. This does not acknowledge the complexity of children's early learning and development and certainly does not do justice to the skills required of their educators.

Take for example childminders. Parents do not simply enter into a business arrangement which deals only with hours and rates of pay. As Ferri (1992) has shown, the reality is much more complex. The childminder needs to understand and make provision for the particular needs of each child. Childminders and parents also need to discuss their views about child rearing so that common ground and approaches can ideally be established in order to provide stability and continuity. Parents need to be clear about what it is they want and expect from childminders, and they in turn must be articulate about what they offer. They also need interpersonal, managerial and business skills, as well as sensitivity, patience, understanding and the knowledge required for successful practice.

Similar principles are relevant to group day-care settings. The staff need information about children as individuals as well as their professional knowledge about child development and early learning. Sometimes, the values and attitudes of staff may clash with those of the parent and vice versa, giving rise to potentially stressful situations, all of which need to be worked out within the different contexts. This requires professional and managerial skills, not just an extended mothering role.

The status of early years teachers in general and nursery teachers in particular is generally regarded as lower than that of teachers of older children (David, 1990; Anning, 1991). However, they need far more than motherly intuition. Nursery teachers work alongside nursery nurses and are required to have managerial skills in order to develop a team-work approach. They need to negotiate roles and responsibilities, identify individual strengths, deploy each adult effectively and be prepared to change and adapt practice on an ongoing basis. In addition, they have to plan the learning environment and manage resources, train students and liaise with parents and other professionals. They also have to plan, implement and evaluate the curriculum, assess children's learning, and be accountable for their provision to parents, colleagues, governors, advisers and inspectors. If a nursery teacher had similar levels of responsibility in industry or commerce, but was dealing with large groups of adults rather than children, the salary and status would be much higher.

The educative role of all adults who work with the under-fives is of central importance to their learning and development. It is present at different levels, and may be expressed in different ways according to circumstances, needs and the age of the child. How adults perceive their role, their intentions and their practice is fundamental to the quality of their provision and their interactions with children. Some examples may serve to illustrate this point.

At a multi-disciplinary seminar participants were asked to

give examples of what they considered to be positive aspects of their practice. One person working in a day nursery related how a 3-year-old had started the day distressed and she had spent the entire morning cuddling him to make him feel better. She saw this as good practice because she felt it was what a parent would do, and the nursery aimed to offer provision which was an extension of home and family life. Now, there is nothing wrong with appropriate physical contact but it is questionable whether this was the only, or indeed the best, strategy for coping with this child's distress. The adult was providing care, but was this educational? A more dynamic approach might have been to encourage the child to talk about his feelings, to establish some strategies for coping, perhaps enable him to plan some activities, regain some control and develop his sense of competence. It is doubtful whether a parent would spend such a long time cuddling a child without at least trying to divert his or her attention in order to help him or her out of a distressed state. This particular adult was also responsible for a group of eight children who, presumably, did not have much of her attention for that morning.

A family centre in the north of England established a prominent role in the local community with parent and adult-education classes, keep fit, a lunch club for senior citizens, and drop-in facilities for health checks and advice. The centre also offered full- and part-time day care, but this seemed to receive less priority than the other facilities. There was little involvement between the adults and children, few resources, the environment lacked interest with no evidence of the children's work and the sand, water and painting areas were not used because they got too messy. The children were under-occupied and there was little concern with planned activities or experiences. This is not a typical example of day-care provision, but serves to illustrate how poor practice can result from inadequate management, diverse priorities and failure to acknowledge the importance of providing education as well as care. Braun (1992, p. 181) has cautioned against an approach where working with parents assumes a life of its own and the activities provided have a tenuous link to the welfare of children.

The importance of the adult's role in day-care settings is outlined in Hennessy *et al.* (1992). They reported that the frequency and type of adult–child interactions were influential in promoting language development, particularly if they were based on real conversations and exchanges of information rather than just giving instructions. Responsiveness, positive interactions and access to stimulating toys and educational materials were also regarded as helping to stimulate cognitive development.

Purposes and practice also vary in maintained nursery schools and classes. A study by Smith (1992) showed that nursery teachers held different beliefs about planning the curriculum, the daily routine and the roles and responsibilities of the adults in the team. In one nursery, the session began with all the children sitting on chairs in a circle, responding to a teacher-initiated activity for learning about shape, colour and size. This was followed by a period of free play with resources selected by the teacher and no involvement from the adults other than a supervisory role. Curriculum planning was based on language, maths, art and imaginative play. The teacher worked with small groups of children on specific tasks such as sorting, matching and pencil-control activities. The nursery nurse supervised the sand and water area at the same time as organizing an art activity. The children all sat together for snacks followed by outdoor play and a story before home time.

In another nursery parents were encouraged to read books with their children before the start of the session in a small library area. The room was organized so that children were able to select resources and have a free choice of activities, indoors and outdoors, according to the weather. Creative and art activities were available each day, planned by either the teacher or the nursery nurse. Each adult was responsible for an area of the room and rotated story-telling and supervising snack time. They allowed a long period of time for self-chosen activities with the adults involving themselves in response to the children's actions and interactions. Curriculum planning was based on the nine areas of learning and experience (DES, 1985/1989) with an integrating theme which changed every four to six weeks. Whilst working on the theme of animals the children had visited a farm, planned a teddy bears' picnic and brought in an assortment of pets, and were caring for a broody hen.

These two examples demonstrate that the teachers held different beliefs about how children learn and how that learning was best promoted in a nursery setting. This highlights the significance of the adult's role in stimulating thinking, learning, language, social competence and physical skills to enable children to develop fully and successfully. This holds true for children of all ages and in all settings which has implications for those who work with the under-fives. They need to be more than just 'a fit person' in order to fulfil their roles successfully. Educating young children is not just about sand and water play, a well-resourced home corner or learning to be independent. It is also about forming minds, attitudes and behaviour which will contribute towards the development of a more equitable society. Developing anti-racist, anti-sexist attitudes and anti-discriminatory practices requires a holistic approach to the curriculum and presents intellectual challenges and choices to under-fives workers. The breadth and complexity of their roles should not be underestimated, nor should the knowledge, skills and aptitudes they require in order to be successful practitioners.

Parents as partners

We have seen how parentcraft classes, family-support services and liaison between parents and pre-school settings have been an important aspect of provision from the beginning of the twentieth century. Originally this was based on the notion of parents as learners who needed expert guidance from early childhood specialists about child development and appropriate child-rearing practices. However, the emphasis has widened to include a more positive view of parents as teachers and their role as partners in the educational process.

Powell (1991, p. 91) has argued that parental involvement can serve different purposes which can be defined as three areas of anticipated outcomes. First, it is assumed that child competence will be enhanced. Second, that parents' self-development will be enhanced, particularly where there is shared power and mutual respect. Third, that the responsiveness and resourcefulness of pre-school provision will be increased. These views have been a feature of many early childhood programmes developed in America and appear to have had a significant influence on performance, attitudes and expectations.

In Britain parental involvement varies in type and extent, according to the different pre-school settings and individual family circumstances. For example, playgroup provision was initiated by parents. The PPA constitution states as its aim:

> To promote community situations in which parents can with growing enjoyment and confidence make the best use of their own knowledge and resources in the development of their children and themselves.

They are usually responsible for their management and organization, and act as leaders and helpers. Parents may also help in nursery schools and classes and in reception classes under the direction of the teacher. They fulfil an important role as fundraisers and, increasingly, as advocates for the development and provision of services. Parents are finding a stronger political voice and are becoming increasingly articulate about the needs of children.

Pugh has argued that liaison and involvement are particularly important for children with special educational needs. Parents have tended to be viewed as passive receivers of services, but they may derive more benefit from developing a relationship with adults who share responsibility for their children and greater involvement in planning and determining services:

> ... if parents were enabled to contribute to as well as receive services, thus building on their skills and developing their self-

confidence, this would provide a firmer base for a more equal relationship between them and professional workers. (1987, p. 176)

Such a model shifts the emphasis from parental involvement to parental partnership. This suggests a sharing of power, resources, knowledge and decision-making between parents and professionals which demands a change in attitudes based on a two-way process (Pugh, 1987, p. 170). Braun (1992, p. 180) outlined some of the problems involved in working with parents, particularly where there are different and sometimes conflicting views, ideas and values: '... for partnership to work, staff need to make efforts to build relationships and to value what the parents bring and who they are'.

Parents need to acknowledge the importance of their role as a child's first educators and not automatically abdicate their responsibility once a child enters a pre-school or school setting. Dowling (1992) has argued that where teachers do not have a high expectation of the parent's role, there is a danger of a self-fulfilling prophecy. Also, parents who do not have a stake in their children's early education place a heavy responsibility on the nursery or school to succeed alone. This implies that teachers and all workers in under-fives settings should work towards shared responsibility and mutual understanding. But how can this be achieved?

There are many strategies for involvement, particularly in the maintained sector, as shown by the variety of different policies developed by schools. Many nursery and reception teachers have a programme of home visiting and shared record-keeping systems. Schools may also provide information about the curriculum, encouraging parental interest and support and helping to make connections between what children learn at home and in school. Some pre-school settings also provide toy and book libraries as well as specially designed packs or boxes which contain a variety of activities for parents to do at home with their children.

At a nursery school in Plymouth, the role of parents and carers was highly valued, with a strong philosophy of partnership. The teachers introduced schemes for paired maths, science and literacy. Based on close observations of children, they designed activities for them to do at home with their parents. These created opportunities to consolidate the child's knowledge and for further development of skills and concepts. In this scheme parents return the activity a week later with feedback to the staff. The children share with their group what they have achieved at home. A policy of support for parents with literacy problems ensures that all are able to participate. The paired schemes promote extension of the children's ideas generated through play both at home and in school. The staff demonstrate that they recognize and value the role of parents as educators and are able to give sensitive guidance to those who find it difficult to support their child's learning at home. Such initiatives provide a two-way flow of information and help to develop a partnership approach based on shared interest in children's ways of thinking, learning and understanding.

These examples demonstrate the shift of emphasis from parents as learners to parents as teachers. It is often the case that parents do not recognize how much teaching they do precisely because it comes under the umbrella term of parenting. The importance of the 'parent as teacher' role was emphasized by Tizard and Hughes (1984). This study focused on working-class mothers and their daughters and contrasted the children's experiences at home and in school. Although this was a narrow sample, the study revealed the richness and variety of conversations which took place in the home and challenged the assumption that working-class children had impoverished backgrounds and experiences. There were many educational exchanges and incidental teaching which arose from the children's interests and activities:

> A notable feature of learning at home was the large amount of general knowledge that the children were given, especially in relation to the ordinary everyday events of living in a family. The children were particularly interested in people, their motivations and activities, and much of the knowledge that their mothers gave them was concerned with the social world. (p. 99)

It must be remembered that not all parents are able or willing to be closely involved with their child's education. For every set of opportunities, there is often a set of obstacles. Some may lack the skills or confidence to establish relationships with other adults in pre-school settings, particularly if they are living in stressed or difficult circumstances, or if they have had negative experiences at school themselves. Involvement is also problematic for parents who work and may not have direct contact with the settings attended by their child. These competing factors cannot always be balanced in perfect harmony for the benefit of children, their families and other involved adults. It is all too easy for parents to be burdened with additional guilt if they do not live up to a mythical ideal. It is also important to recognize the limitations on the time, energy and expertise of those who work with the under-fives. They cannot be all things to all people since this may result in a dilution of priorities and a thin spread of expertise over a wide range of problems.

This underlines the importance of family-support services based on effective co-ordination and co-operation between the different departments and adequate information to parents about what is offered and how it can be accessed. Services need to be complementary rather than just compensatory so that parents can develop their role as educators and help to enhance the benefits of pre-school provision.

In this chapter we have established that pre-school education can increase children's potential and have examined the significance of parents and practitioners in this process. It has also been argued that an influential factor in the effectiveness of pre-school provision is the type of curriculum offered to children. The next chapter will review current knowledge and understanding about how young children learn and will relate this to what is an appropriate curriculum for the under-fives.

Chapter 6

A CURRICULUM FOR THE UNDER-FIVES

This chapter begins with a clarification of what is meant by the term curriculum and how this is relevant to the under-fives in all settings and the home. First I will consider the different elements in the structure of the curriculum and outline a range of approaches to curriculum planning for this age group. Each will be critically examined in terms of the theoretical underpinning and implications for practice. I will go on to examine the key features for success in determining curriculum content. The intention in this chapter is to give an overview of theory and practice to stimulate informed consideration of what constitutes an appropriate curriculum for the under-fives.

Towards a definition

For many people, the term curriculum may seem more relevant to the junior or secondary years, with a set timetable, different subjects and a clearly defined body of knowledge to be imparted at different ages within a school context. The notion of a curriculum for the under-fives, and particularly for the under-threes, has been more elusive. As noted earlier in this book the pioneering work of Susan Isaacs, Margaret McMillan, Rudolf Steiner and Maria Montessori became increasingly influential in developing specially designed curricula based on the development, needs and interests of young children (Bruce, 1987; Anning, 1991). The work of these and other pioneers helped to change prevailing views about childhood so that it came to be regarded as a period in its own right, and not merely as a form of immature adulthood or preparation for adult life. Accordingly it was seen as deserving of educational provision which was designed with the particular needs and interests of young children in mind.

There has never been a commonly agreed or centrally defined curriculum for the under-fives. The range of approaches and aims in different settings has contributed to the vulnerability of the under-fives sector, adding to the overall picture of confusion, lack of consistency and commonly agreed aims and purposes. However, a greater degree of clarity has emerged during the last ten years, based on theory, research and government reports. These support the view that a curriculum for the under-fives is both realistic and desirable. Moreover, recent thinking has broadened the concept of curriculum to link children's home experiences with other settings and with school. The definition offered by Drummond, Lally and Pugh (1989, p. 11) encompasses this view. They state that a curriculum for young children includes:

- all the opportunities for learning and development that are made available to young children;
- the activities, attitudes and behaviour that are planned, encouraged, tolerated or ignored;
- the way the room is organized and the routines following by adults and children;
- the part adults take in organizing, directing, influencing and joining in what the children do;
- the extent to which parents are involved in each of the above.

Rouse and Griffin (1992, p. 138) give a complementary definition of curriculum for the under-threes:

- all the activities and experiences provided for babies and toddlers by educators;
- all the activities children devise for themselves;
- the gestures, vocalizations and language that educators use to communicate with children and all the language they use with each other;
- all that children see, touch, hear, taste and smell in the environment around them.

81

Teachers and other under-fives specialists I have worked with on in-service courses have found these to be thought-provoking definitions since they are relevant to all age groups across different settings. They also link the curriculum that is planned with the curriculum that is actually experienced by the children, encouraging adults to think critically about their values, roles and attitudes as well as the underlying purposes of the activities and experiences offered. The term 'educator' can be applied to adults in different settings as well as parents, thus promoting the view that everybody has a significant role to play in children's education. Furthermore, these definitions acknowledge that, as in later phases of schooling, a curriculum for the under-fives has both structure and content and is not just an ad hoc, chaotic jumble of activities and experiences. Structure and content will now be explored more fully.

The structure of the curriculum

This is comprised of five main elements – planning, organization, implementation, assessment and evaluation. Each element warrants careful consideration in relation to the age of the children and the particular setting, but all are interlinked and interdependent. Starting points for planning will vary according to each setting, which 'model' or approach is used, the age and number of children, the available space, length of session and number of adults. Planning for a playgroup session in a church hall with no outdoor space presents different challenges to planning for 3- to 5-year-olds in a purpose-built nursery school. The skill lies in making the best of what is available, even if that is not ideal or even desirable.

Adults should also take into account gender, race and children with special educational needs. Planning for equality of opportunity should receive a high priority so that all children can benefit fully from the curriculum offered. First, all children need to feel that their identity and culture is valued. Second, children need to understand differences and similarities, and to develop respect and acceptance. Research studies have shown that by the age of 3 children are already beginning to develop sexist and racist attitudes. In one nursery session, the children were planning what they intended to do on the large apparatus in the school hall. Helen said she planned to climb right to the top of the wall bars. Wayne immediately retorted, 'Don't be silly, you can't do that 'cos girls aren't strong enough. Only boys can go to the top.' Following this remark, I structured part of the session so that both boys and girls demonstrated their climbing skills. It is important that stereotyped views about race, gender and disability are actively challenged and that positive images and role models are given.

Planning for children with special educational needs also requires careful consideration. It is a sad indictment that many children with a physical disability may be denied access to any form of provision if buildings and facilities are unsuitable or inadequate. Sometimes, creativity and flexibility can overcome obstacles. John, aged 3, entered a nursery class sited in a former infant classroom. He suffered from cerebral palsy, had considerable difficulty co-ordinating his movements and would frequently crash into furniture or trip over children and equipment. It was decided that removing some of the furniture would create wider spaces for John to negotiate his way around. In the event, the changes proved beneficial to all the children, liberating more space for the role play and block play areas. Because of his disability, some of the children (particularly the girls) wanted to mother John, often casting him in the role of baby in their play and pushing him around the room or playground in the wooden pram. This meant that John was not developing his social or physical skills, and the other children needed to become more aware of his abilities rather than his disabilities. Again this necessitated intervention on the part of the adults so that John could demonstrate his progress and capabilities in different situations.

Curriculum planning should take account of breadth, balance, progression, differentiation and continuity. In practice this means offering a wide range of activities and experiences which are appropriate to the children. Many of these will be based on different types of play. It must be remembered that play in itself does not constitute a curriculum and there are many other ways in which children can learn which are equally valuable. Breadth and balance can also be achieved by creative planning. Old favourites such as sand, water and dough can be structured to provide a wide range of learning experiences. If children always have the same tools and equipment, their activity may become repetitive and stereotyped. For example, rolling pins and cutters with dough tend to encourage children (mostly girls) to make endless trays of cakes. More exciting possibilities are opened up if different equipment is added – blunt knives, a potato masher, garlic press, colander, items for modelling and printing – or if the texture of the dough is varied by the addition of sand, dried pulses or pea gravel.

Progression means that children should have opportunities to build on existing skills and knowledge, and be presented with new challenges. It is difficult to achieve progression in practice. Children do not learn in an ordered, simple, consistent fashion. Achieving real progression demands that adults are very finely tuned in to ongoing needs and interests, as well as having the knowledge and skills to support learning. It is important to have a wide range of resources available. For example, a variety of jigsaws ranging from inset trays to interlocking puzzles, different construction equipment to provide new challenges, varied opportunities for role play which reflect and widen children's knowledge of the real world.

Differentiation means that adults should take into account the needs of individual children, particularly those with special educational needs, and adapt the curriculum accordingly. We have already seen how reorganizing the room helped John. He also benefited from equipment loaned from the special needs support service such as pencil grips and plastic mats to provide a non-slip surface for paper and equipment. Again, adults need to think carefully about the selection of equipment, rules, routines and their role.

Organization and implementation of the curriculum are influenced by a range of factors: what activities and experiences will be provided; where these will be sited for maximum benefit; how much time will be allocated to the different activities; the role of the adults; the balance between child-chosen and adult-directed activities. These are the sorts of decisions which adults must make in all settings whatever the age group. For example, changing a baby's nappy can be regarded as a basic necessity for comfort, hygiene and welfare. At another level it can become an opportunity for interaction between the adult and child, with eye contact and 'conversational' exchanges which form part of the bonding and learning process. This involves consideration of the baby's needs, time management and informed perceptions of the adult's role. Childminders also make conscious decisions about how the day will be organized and what sort of activities are considered to be educationally worthwhile. It is not in their personal or professional interests to have bored, fractious or under-stimulated children.

The assessment and evaluation processes provide vital feedback on how the curriculum is experienced by the children and the implications for further planning and organization. It can be argued that assessment and evaluation are the real starting points for curriculum planning to ensure that the content is actually relevant to the perceived needs and interests of the childen. Assessment serves two broad purposes. First, as a way of tracking children's progress and development. Second, as a way of demonstrating accountability to parents, governors, the local authority and other interested parties. The evaluation process draws upon assessment to provide the evidence against which to review the curriculum, teaching styles, learning opportunities and educational achievements (Drummond, 1993). If used thoughtfully and effectively assessment and evaluation create a continuous cycle of feedback and feedforward which can help adults to achieve that fine-tuning process. This is essentially the bedrock of a successful, stimulating curriculum which meets the needs not just of a broad age group but of individual learners.

The examples given here demonstrate the interdependence

of the five elements which make up the structure of the curriculum, and ways in which they are relevant to all under-fives settings. The structure acts as a framework for the actual content. How the content is defined and organized involves another set of complex decisions and actions.

The content of the curriculum

This is determined by what is considered to be educationally worthwhile. Of course, educationalists, theorists, philosophers and politicians have different views about this. Deciding what is educationally worthwhile involves value judgements about what is valuable to the child in the immediate term, what is valuable to society in the longer term, and which forms of knowledge are important. Education, learning and development are lifelong processes. Therefore it is important that children should have positive attitudes and flexible approaches to learning which serve their current and future needs.

Broadly speaking, content is based upon the development of knowledge, skills, understanding, values and attitudes. This should ideally take place in an environment which is safe, secure and familiar but at the same time challenging, stimulating and enabling. Adults need to recognize that all children bring with them experiences gained at home and in the community so that learning and development are enhanced through a process of building on the child's existing knowledge and competences. The sorts of activities and experiences selected should support and extend learning in the three domains or areas of development:

1. Cognitive – all the skills and processes involved in learning, understanding and thinking.
   For example, concentration, problem-solving, creativity, imagination, exploration, investigation, understanding cause and effect, language, concept formation.

2. Psycho-motor – all aspects of physical development:
   Fine motor – use of hands, fingers and fingertips, hand/eye co-ordination.

For example, grasping, holding and letting go, crayoning, painting, cutting out, turning the pages of a book.

Gross motor – large body movements.

For example, sitting, standing, turning, twisting, balancing, controlled movement of head, trunk and limbs in relation to space.

Locomotor – large body movements involving travelling and awareness of space.

For example, crawling, running, climbing, walking, hopping, skipping, jumping.

3. Socio-affective – all the skills and processes involved in learning a repertoire of appropriate behaviours, making relationships, social interaction, expressing and controlling emotion, developing a sense of self, understanding the needs of others.

The three domains should not be seen as separate but as a complex, interlinking framework. For example, a child on a climbing frame is using gross motor skills, but at the same time will be making decisions about where to place hands and feet, how to reach a specific point, assessing whether he or she has the capabilities (motivation, skill, sense of personal competence) to meet the challenge. Similarly, many of the skills and concepts involved in learning to read are acquired long before children start school. These include learning to handle a book, starting the right way up and at the beginning, being able to turn the pages, understanding that a book includes print and/or pictures and that both can convey a range of meanings – stories, information, poems, recipes, jokes, and so forth.

The starting points for selecting and organizing content vary between settings. Some of the approaches used may be 'home grown', reflecting the knowledge and experience of the adult in charge. Others may be based on set curriculum models – clearly defined programmes or local authority guidelines. In general, adults use a combination of their own approaches and elements of other curriculum models to suit their own particular circumstances and beliefs. I will now give a brief outline of some of these models and discuss their theoretical underpinning, strengths and weaknesses.

Areas of learning and experience

In a report published in 1989 on 'The Education of Children under Five,' HMI recommended that curriculum planning should be based on nine areas of learning and experience:

Aesthetic and Creative
Human and Social
Linguistic and Literary
Mathematical
Moral
Physical
Scientific
Spiritual
Technological

It was acknowledged that these were not separate and that knowledge, skills and understanding could be combined in a variety of ways across the nine areas. This is known as an integrated or cross-curricular approach to planning. The intention was to encourage teachers and other under-fives workers to adopt a clearly defined framework for the curriculum to ensure breadth, balance and differentiation for children with special educational needs, and to promote equal opportunities. The report stated the importance of developing high-quality educational opportunities, maximizing the potential for learning and development characteristic of this age group and providing a sound basis for later educational attainment. Concern was also expressed about developing cohesive approaches to planning, assessment and effective teaching.

The report argued that pre-school settings should not be a hot-house forcing-ground or set up barriers to further achievement by underestimating children's capabilities and providing compensatory education which focused on emotional rather than cognitive development. This reflected advances in theories of children's learning which emphasized the influence of the social contexts in which learning takes place, the values, attitudes and beliefs of the home and pre-school environments, adult support and interaction, and the powerful emotional factors involved in learning.

The report promoted a more rigorous approach which upheld the value of play but at the same time acknowledged the importance of other activities such as using the local environment, visits to places of interest, inviting visitors to talk about their jobs as a stimulus to role play and extending knowledge of the real world. Some of the examples of good practice give an indication of what can be achieved by young children with creative, purposeful planning. This also brought into focus the fact that settings which concentrate on caring, nurturing and protecting children can be benign and ineffective learning environments.

Another purpose of this report was to develop continuity and progression with later phases of schooling in view of the subject-based approach of the National Curriculum. Some nursery teachers felt marginalized or threatened by the National Curriculum and were unsure whether or how it would influence their practice. This report at least sought to bridge that gap and to open up the dialogue between the different phases of schooling.

Starting with Quality – the Rumbold Report

This report adopted the nine areas of learning and experience as a broad framework, and acknowledged that different aspects may be grouped together. Of greater significance was that

> the curriculum should be coherent in terms of the child's existing knowledge, understanding and skills, and that it should be experienced in an environment which fosters the development of social relationships and positive attitudes to learning and behaviour. (DES, 1990, p. 9)

Although the wide variations between settings were acknowledged, the report recommended that all staff should have a clear view of the curriculum framework and should develop effective team approaches to planning, organization, implementation, assessment and evaluation. Other factors which were regarded as essential in ensuring quality for the under-fives were the role of the adult; partnership with parents; continuity and progression; the learning environment; co-ordination between services and providers; education, training and support for under-fives workers.

Skills-based planning

Curtis (1986) devised a curriculum for the pre-school child based on a range of skills and competences. These are the development of:

Self-awareness
Social skills
Cultural awareness skills
Communication skills (through language, music, movement, dance, art)
Motor and perceptual skills
Analytical and problem-solving skills
Aesthetic and creative awareness

Each of these areas is broken down into further components which give breadth and balance to the curriculum. For example, analytical and problem-solving skills include observation, classification, seriation (ordering), number, spatial relations, temporal awareness and understanding the relationship between cause and effect. Developing curiosity and intrinsic motivation are seen as fundamental to learning in all the areas.

Curtis argued that activities and experiences in themselves do not always lead to learning. Children can be relatively easily occupied at low-level, repetitive tasks in which they practise skills but do not learn new concepts or extend their current thinking. It is much more demanding for adults to provide opportunities and challenges which stimulate learning in a thoughtfully planned and well-resourced environment. This links what should be learned (the knowledge, skills, concepts, values and attitudes) with how it should be learned.

The Highscope curriculum

This originated in America during the 1960s but was informed by some of the best nursery practice in Britain (Hohmann *et al.*, 1979). It is known as a 'cognitively oriented' curriculum and was evolved in response to the polarized and inadequate programmes prevalent at that time. In theoretical terms it was originally based on the work of Jean Piaget, the Swiss psychologist. Piaget argued that children are active learners who need direct, first-hand experience and a wide variety of stimuli. In his view, children are like lone scientists, working progressively to construct layers of understanding, skills and knowledge. This is seen as an individual process in which the child selects activities and experiences which reflect current interests or, to use Piaget's term, 'schemas'. This is known as a constructivist theory of learning.

The Highscope curriculum is organized around key experiences:

Social development
Representation
Language
Classification
Seriation
Number
Space
Time
Movement and physical development

Adults use these to guide them in observing, understanding and supporting children's interests and emerging abilities. Resources are selected and the room organized in order to allow self-chosen activities based on a 'plan–do–review' sequence. The children are encouraged to plan their own activities and goals, to carry out their plan and to review it at the end of the session. The review is seen as an important aspect of the curriculum, encouraging children to show the group what they have made or relate what they have done, and how this was achieved, and to identify their own learning and thought processes (metacognition). The plan–do–review sequence gives children choice and autonomy. The role of the teacher is to negotiate with the child the areas to be visited and activities to be undertaken, then to act as enabler and facilitator in that process, where appropriate.

The Highscope curriculum was introduced into Britain during the 1980s. This approach has many supporters – some are evangelical in their praise, particularly about the ways in which Highscope promotes independence and autonomy, encourages children to think for themselves, make decisions and take control of their own learning. However, critics have questioned the emphasis on the individualized nature of learning which Highscope promotes. Opportunities for collaborative play can be reduced, potentially undervaluing the importance of developing relationships and vital social skills such as negotiation, co-operation, sharing, initiating and responding. One nursery headteacher told me that she had rejected Highscope for this reason. She gave examples of how children often formulate their plans on the way to school and needed sustained periods of time for putting them into action.

There is a danger that describing a curriculum model as 'cognitively oriented' implies that other models have different emphases and may be concerned with non-cognitive aims such as social and emotional development. But, as noted above, the three areas of development are inextricably linked. Learning about rules, roles, relationships and one's place in the world all involve conceptual thinking and understanding, just as much as learning about maths, science or language. This is an important point, in view of the need to bridge the traditional care and education divide.

The Highscope curriculum is quite structured in terms of the daily timetable, the role of the adults and the methods for achieving the goals set by the programme. Many nursery practitioners have found this to be at odds with the British tradition of free play. There is always a danger with any curriculum model, particularly one which combines a distinctive philosophy with a clearly defined structure, that the programme becomes more important than the children. When I first saw Highscope in action in a nursery class in 1987 I was struck by the rigidity of the timetable and the number of changes between the different elements. Paradoxically, this allowed only a short period of time, forty minutes out of a two and a half hour session, for the children to carry out their plans. However, evaluations of the Highscope programme here suggest that teachers and other adults have taken specific elements and adapted these to their own practice rather than adhering rigidly to the framework. More recent guidelines for Highscope in this country have outlined a broader theoretical base than the original manual (Brown, 1992) and have affirmed the importance of social interaction and the adult's role.

It is questionable just how independent and autonomous children can be as learners. Learning involves challenge and change, pain and pleasure, success and failure. It is a complex interweaving of skills, processes, attitudes and dispositions. However skilled we are, even as adults, learning is often facilitated by interaction with more knowledgeable others who can provide appropriate assistance. Providing the right support at the right time is particularly important for children as they have less knowledge and experience on which to build.

The work of other psychologists, notably Jerome Bruner and Lev Vygotsky, offers some alternative theories of learning in early childhood. They both support the view that children are active learners and that knowledge has to be constructed rather than handed down. However, they place greater emphasis on the importance of talk and social interaction with other children and adults.

Appropriate questioning, meaningful dialogue, sensitive intervention and assistance all provide a framework or scaffold to support and extend learning. Children construct knowledge and understanding through their own actions and interactions with their environment and significant others. This is known as a social-constructivist theory of learning.

Giving status to children's own plans and interests is fundamental to an effective curriculum since it allows adults to
identify how children are learning and thinking. Providing
frameworks and strategies to support, extend and enhance
learning are equally important.

Areas of development

Some settings plan activities based on the areas of development outlined above – cognitive, psycho-motor, socio-affective.
Sometimes these are referred to differently – physical, intellectual, emotional and social (PIES) – but they are essentially
the same. For the under-twos this can be a useful starting
point, particularly since adults tend to exert more control in
selecting appropriate experiences, initiating play and stimulating interactions. Because children's development at this age
is rapid, their needs change on a month-by-month basis.
Adults need to keep pace with these changes, structuring
provision, routines and their roles accordingly.

For older children, however, this can be a limited approach
to planning. In some settings, I have seen daily plans which
outline which activities will be provided (if it's Monday, it's
Lego), but without a clear rationale for the intended learning,
possible outcomes or consideration of the children's ongoing
interests. In this approach, it is the adults who select the
activities and experiences leaving little room for children's
choices and decisions. Environments which are over-struc-
tured can lead to repetitive, low-level play which does not
challenge children sufficiently or fully develop their potential.

A schematic approach

In this approach, adults base the curriculum offered on their
close observations of children's learning, their ongoing
interests, concerns and problems. A schema is an individualized pattern of thinking, learning and action. These patterns
can be repeated across a range of different experiences and
activities, leading children towards categorizing, classifying,
establishing relationships, understanding causes and effects,
actions and reactions. Athey (1990) sees schemas as the core

of a child's developing mind and the basis of intellectual growth, a means by which children make sense of their environment and their place within it.

A nursery teacher became interested in schemas and started to observe target children closely to see if she could become skilled in 'schema spotting'. She noticed that Ben, aged 4, was interested in transport. He enjoyed making layouts with Brio, Duplo and Playmobil, returning to these activities daily. In his drawings and paintings, Ben represented his understanding in similar ways – a long straight line with intersecting lines across the bottom of the page, with rectangles, squares and triangles above. Through discussion, the teacher learnt that these represented a railway line, a bus to take people to the station and all the buildings they passed. Ben was combing his knowledge of the real world in his play, demonstrating experience, imagination and representation. This can also be seen as an important stage in geographical development – spatial awareness, understanding relationships between people and their environment, making and reading maps. The teacher was able to extend Ben's interests by providing books and pictures, talking about journeys and transport and providing opportunities for developing his ability to make plans and maps.

Through close observation of children at home and in school, Athey argues that adults can identify children's schemas in their patterns of play and behaviour, through their language and representations – models, layouts, drawings, paintings. Children repeat and rehearse their schemas in many different forms. Patterns can be identified in babies, toddlers and young children, thus offering adults important insights into a child's learning and development. By knowing children's ongoing interests, parents and staff can achieve that process of fine-tuning in which the curriculum is matched to individual needs and is not determined exclusively by an adult's view of what should be learned, when and how.

One of the difficulties of this approach is that it appears to demand an individually designed learning programme for every child. For a childminder or leader of a small home-based playgroup, this might be manageable. For a teacher with thirty or more 4-year-olds in a reception class, this would be more problematic. However, groups of children often have similar interests and 'cognitive concerns' so that adults can still achieve a balance between planning for the whole class, small groups and individuals. The skill lies in close observation and systems of assessment and evaluation which provide informed feedback about the effectiveness of the curriculum offered.

For children with special educational needs, schema spotting can be a way of understanding what each child can do, forming a foundation for further learning. All too often we become obsessed with developmental norms as if all children conform to set patterns. Children with developmental delay or disability can thus be seen in terms of their deficits rather than their abilities. Understanding schemas is a way of understanding learning – what Drummond (1993) has described as 'getting inside a child's head'.

This approach is also valuable for children from different cultural and linguistic backgrounds who may be learning English as a second language. Close observation of children can tell us a lot about the influences of different cultures, religious beliefs and child-rearing practices. This enables adults to respond to the needs of children and their families, ensuring that the curriculum offered recognizes, values and respects diversity and reflects the multiracial, multicultural society in which we live.

A topic/thematic approach

This is often favoured by teachers and nursery nurses since it provides a way of integrating the different subject areas, as well as promoting breadth and balance. In this model, a theme such as Ourselves, Light and Dark, Colour, Transport is chosen and may last from a fortnight to half a term. Activities and experiences are organized to promote knowledge, skills and understanding which are linked to the theme and enable children to make connections and relationships. For example, one nursery school was working on the theme of

'Indoors and Outdoors' during the summer term. The overall plan or 'topic web' was made available to parents, encouraging them to contribute and make connections with the children's experiences at home. One aspect of the theme concentrated on bees. A beekeeper visited the nursery and talked about his work. He brought some of his equipment and a real honey-comb. The children tasted honey, learnt about hexagons and how they fit together, did drawings and paintings and made models of bees, and learnt about the sounds they make, polli-nation, bee-friendly habitats and their life cycle. The role-play area was turned into a garden centre with real artefacts – seeds, compost, seed catalogues, tools and equipment. The children also had an outside area for growing things. The staff introduced poems, stories, songs and music about bees as well as providing information books and pictures. The theme was extended to include other insects, plants and different habitats.

The advantage of this model is that it focuses attention on the learning that is intended and provides a wide range of experiences which children might not otherwise have. How-ever, staff still need to ensure that there is time and space for the children to develop and extend their own interests and ideas. Planned activities often lead to unplanned develop-ments. If the theme is too slavishly adhered to, adult choice and adult-led activities may predominate. Too much direc-tion and intervention can be as problematic as too little. As with other models, the adults need time to observe the children and evaluate how the curriculum is being received. They then need to support, extend and, where necessary, 'go with the flow' of the children's responses and reactions.

National Curriculum planning

As noted earlier, the introduction of the National Curriculum has exerted some downward pressure on the under-fives, par-ticularly in nursery schools and classes. Some have already adopted 'subject-based' planning with an indication of how the nursery curriculum is meeting the Attainment Targets at Key Stage 1 of the National Curriculum. There are two ways of looking at this particular approach. Nursery staff need to demonstrate areas of overlap and complementarity. This has enabled many teachers to articulate the relevance, value and strength of a good nursery curriculum, particularly in terms of developing continuity between the phases. Also, there has been a tendency in the past to use fairly loose terms about what goes on in early childhood education – play, first-hand experience, active learning, educating the whole child. All of these may have different meanings to different people and can be difficult to define in a rigorous and systematic manner. Using a subject-based approach helps to ensure breadth and acknowledges that many of the skills and concepts which children learn in the pre-school years are subject specific. For example, a child playing in the water tray may not be described as doing science. But many aspects of the activity are scientific in that it provides opportunities for observation, investigation, experimentation, formulating hypotheses, making predictions, testing and discovering the properties of water. These processes lead to concept formation about float-ing and sinking, weight, mass and volume.

It is important for staff in pre-school settings to be aware of the requirements of the National Curriculum, particularly since many of the Statements of Attainment for Level 1 are well within the capabilities of 4-year-olds. This also helps to establish continuity and progression. However, this does not imply that this model should be used exclusively, or that formal, didactic methods of teaching should be adopted with the under-fives. There is widespread concern that the National Curriculum, along with standard assessment tasks at 7, has engendered a 'too formal too soon' approach in some pre-school settings, particularly reception classes. This has led to a devaluing of play and an over-prescriptive framework which is not legally applicable to the under-fives. The National Curriculum defines what children over 5 should learn, but it is up to early years practitioners in all settings to ensure that they do not lose sight of how young children learn. Adults' way of teaching must be in harmony with children's ways of thinking, knowing, learning, understanding and doing.

A curriculum for the under-threes

The National Children's Bureau has produced guidelines for good practice for young children in day care (1991). The purposes of the guidelines are to raise awareness of the needs of young children, improve policy and service provision across social services, health, education and the voluntary sector and to support the raising of professional standards of practice. The guidelines cover registration, legal requirements, health and safety, staffing patterns, qualifications and development and working in partnership with parents. The section on policy and practice outlines a curriculum for the under-threes which recognizes that care and education are indivisible and that the role of the adult is fundamental to developing good practice. This applies in all interactions which staff have with young children, whether it is establishing eye contact at nappy changing time, or through attentive engagement alongside a child during play or at mealtimes.

The curriculum includes planning for indoor and outdoor play, local walks and outings. All parts of the day are seen as providing opportunities for children's learning, for example, meal times, personal hygiene, self-help skills, tidying the nursery. Many of these routine tasks are the stuff of everyday family life and can help children in day care not to feel institutionalized. Groupings and relationships are also important in this respect. The guidelines recommend a key-worker system with one adult responsible for a small group of children. In one university family centre, this was developed into a dual key-worker system so that one familiar adult was available if another was absent. Both adults were responsible for greeting each child in the family group, liaising with parents, getting to know each child on an individual basis and planning for needs and interests. The groups remained with their key workers as they got older, providing continuity and stability during those first formative years.

Another important aspect of good practice in day care is the development of children's sense of their own self-worth. The guidelines emphasize the importance of a broad, balanced curriculum which reflects positively the multiracial, multicultural nature of British society. The attitudes of all staff are seen as crucial in promoting equality of opportunity, challenging racism and sexism and enhancing the development of children's self-esteem.

Local authority guidelines

Many local authorities have devised their own guidelines for good practice and curriculum development in different preschool settings. Some cover 3- to 5-year-olds, but increasingly this is being extended to include from birth to 5 or 8, thus reflecting the importance of the whole early years phase. They often include statements of principles to act as a foundation for developing cohesive, broadly-based strategies for development. Many guidelines have adopted the nine areas of learning and experience (HMI, 1985/1989) as a framework for curriculum planning and include child-assessment profiles which are shared with parents and can be transferred between settings. Common themes include the importance of early years education, the value of play, promoting equal opportunities, catering for special educational needs, partnership with parents, continuity and liaison between settings.

Finding a way forward

The foregoing discussion has indicated a complex maze of different approaches and ideas about early learning and curriculum organization. Finding a way through this maze is part of the challenge of working with young children, particularly in view of the importance of the early years in forming positive attitudes towards learning. Clearly there is no single curriculum which can be implemented uniformly in different settings with different age groups. The under-fives are not a homogeneous group. They vary considerably in age, development, needs, aptitudes, behaviour, cultural and social background. They need provision which is tailored accordingly. Developing a curriculum is a complex task which requires consideration of many variables. It should be seen as an organizing framework which provides structure and direction but at the same time can respond to and initiate change. In terms of the content, what children learn should be informed by how they learn and what they already bring with them. Understanding the processes of learning helps to formulate and consolidate the outcomes, providing the scaffolding for further learning.

For young children, a great deal of learning takes place through the various kinds of play activities they engage in at home and in pre-school settings. However play in itself does not constitute a curriculum (Moyles, 1989). It is one of the means by which the curriculum in any organized setting is enacted. There is a tendency to use the term play to cover a whole range of activities and experiences which may have different qualities. Play can be aimless, repetitive, low level, occupying, benign. Play can also be deeply serious, challenging, exciting, demanding, creative, stimulating, innovative. Play can stimulate many kinds of learning in a wide variety of contexts. Children need lots of opportunities for play activities with different materials, objects, toys and games, both indoors and outdoors. They need the space and time to develop long and complex play sequences as they get older. Contrary to popular belief, young children can and do concentrate for long periods when they are intrinsically motivated and engaged on meaningful tasks. Flitting about and milling around are indicative of an inadequate curriculum which provides insufficient challenge and stimulus.

Children also need opportunities to play alone, in pairs or in groups, with children and with adults. There has been a long-standing belief that intervention by adults in children's play is inappropriate because it invades their private worlds. However, there is a difference between intervention, where adults may seek to direct and control children's play, and interaction, where adults play alongside children as partners. An interactionist approach involves reciprocity between adult and child, with the adult using observation and skill to know how and when to prompt, question, give suggestions, demonstrate a skill, aid understanding or assist a child's performance. All are significant aspects of the scaffolding process described earlier. It is also important to know when to stand back and allow a child to struggle, to respect a child's right to privacy and ownership in his or her play, to give praise and recognition for what children put into their play – effort, creativity, imagination, co-operation – not just for a pretty picture, a nice painting or a good model.

An interactionist approach is equally important for babies. From around two months, babies begin to develop interest in the world around them, and particularly in adults. They can engage in social interactions through eye contact and through responding to touch, smell and sound. Early cooing and babbling are now recognized as the first important stages in communication. A baby may not be able to make sense of the words, but can make sense of the interaction with a significant other person. As babies develop their interest in people and then in objects, the first opportunities for play arise – peek-a-boo, turn taking, giving and taking. It is important throughout this stage that adults recognize the significance of this early learning, then support and extend the impetus through further social interaction.

Play can serve many different purposes and needs. Its very scope has made it difficult to define in a systematic manner. This in turn has meant that early childhood educators have found it problematic to defend play as part of the curriculum, particularly in reception classes. If anything, over-emphasizing the value of play has served to undermine early childhood practitioners and trivialize the curriculum, making the job seem far easier than it actually is. The attempts by the Conservative government to deprofessionalize early years teachers in 1993 with the proposed introduction of a 'Mum's Army' reflected in part the lack of understanding of the importance of the early years and the complexity of early learning. If children were only playing, they weren't learning and therefore did not need highly trained adults.

What is needed is a more rigorous examination of the processes which link play and learning, such as exploration, investigation, experimentation, imagination, creativity, motivation, and the sort of play contexts which stimulate learning in its widest sense. The more we understand about learning the more complex the task of teaching appears, and I use the word teaching to include parents and all adults involved in educating the under-fives. The notions of interaction and reciprocity described above indicate the quality of engagement between adults and children which is required to achieve that fine-tuning process. Sometimes the adult will lead, but will then need to be sensitive to the child's interpretation of the adult's intentions and expectations. Sometimes the child will lead, giving adults insights into his or her developing skills and understanding. We cannot leave it all to the child, precisely because of their inexperience as learners. We cannot leave it all to play, because other activities and experiences which adults select can be equally valuable if they are appropriately matched and worthwhile.

Another important aspect of the curriculum is knowing how to structure the environment in order to support learning. Again, structure should not be thought of as a strait-jacket where adults always predetermine what activities are made available and how they should be used. Structure can be an enabling and extending framework supporting choice, engagement and motivation. This approach has the advantage of allowing children more scope for setting their own goals with adults helping to achieve them where appropriate.

The overall framework should allow for a balance between adult-directed and child-chosen activities so that learning, development and the potential of every child can be maximized. For example, a role-play area can be changed regularly to stimulate knowledge and understanding of the real world, of roles, rules and relationships. I have seen many successful examples including a supermarket, café, hairdressers, baby clinic, hospital, fire station, garage, school, office, travel agents, caravan, space station. With imaginative resourcing, children's learning can be extended in challenging, exciting ways.

We also need to acknowledge that educating the under-fives can and should recognize the relevance of subject-based knowledge such as mathematics, science and literacy. Some of this is introduced in an informal way, for example through number, finger play and nursery rhymes, in sand and water play, art and craft. Creative planning and appropriate structures can offer wider opportunities for early learning which enhance the quality of children's play. Understanding the key skills, processes and concepts within the different subject areas can enable adults to strengthen the foundations of early learning and provide meaningful continuity with later phases of schooling. This is also important because of the National Curriculum framework and Standard Assessment Tasks (SATs) at 7. An evaluation of the 1991 SATs found significant differences in the scores in English and Mathematics between children who had had nursery experience and those who had not (Shorrocks, 1992). This again underlines the value of good pre-school provision.

Clearly the type of curriculum offered does matter. The question of whether one curriculum is better than another is problematic given the range of pre-school settings. Of central concern are the features which combine to promote quality of experience and outcomes in all settings. Research both here and in America suggests that the key features for quality and effectiveness include:

- a curriculum which is broad, balanced, developmentally appropriate and culturally relevant;
- clearly defined aims and commonly agreed approaches;
- strategies for assessment and evaluation;
- skilled and knowledgeable adults;
- generous adult:child ratios;
- parental involvement and support;
- parent education programmes, where necessary;
- high quality pre- and in-service training.

The important point is that these can and should feature in all pre-school settings, thus promoting a gradual breakdown of elitism between different groups of adults and types of provision, and eroding the notion that care and education are separate. The quality of educational input must be a distinctive feature of the quality criteria for all forms of provision.

Maintained nursery education is often regarded as providing the best curriculum for 3- to 5-year-olds, based on the expertise of trained teachers and nursery nurses. But even if this became universally available parents would still need the flexibility of other forms of provision. Part of the challenge for the future is to understand how these key features for success and effectiveness can be combined in different settings for the under-fives so that a curriculum which synthesizes high-quality care and education is realizable for all children.

Chapter 7

TOWARDS THE TWENTY-FIRST CENTURY

This book has outlined many of the problems and possibilities, changes and challenges which influence the lives of young children and their families. How these will be addressed over the next few years is very much open to speculation. What is certain is the extent of change required to ensure higher-quality provision for the under-fives which is affordable, accessible, more widely available on a local basis and relevant to the needs of all children and their families. So, do we have cause for cautious optimism, or for more frustrated pessimism? The answer, at least in the short term, is probably both, depending on how we view the past, present and future.

First, on the optimistic side, there are many imperatives to change at different levels. The Children Act has provided a legislative framework which imposes duties and responsibilities on local authorities to safeguard children's rights and instigate a rolling programme of development for services and provision. However, this appears to be targeted predominantly at children in need, rather than the wider needs of all children in society. This narrow focus may in itself not be appropriate if children are channelled into publicly funded forms of provision which focus on care and compensation rather than education and empowerment for children and their families.

We also need to ask whether the Children Act will go as far as it should, given the scale of the problems in the under-fives sector. Currently the valuable information gathered in the review process appears to be of relevance only on a local basis. There is no central government policy or plan to utilize this information to improve the quantity and quality of provision and services in the United Kingdom. Local authorities and employers have consistently called for some central direction through a lead department, perhaps within the Department for Education, with a Minister for Children. This would lend support to local initiatives and commitments. Without this the nature of any future development will continue to be selective and ad hoc.

The question of whether one overall co-ordinating body should assume responsibility for all provision for the under-fives has not been resolved at local government level. Some authorities have already placed this with education, others are operating on a joint-planning basis. This leaves outstanding some of the issues about territorial influence, different approaches and philosophies. Perhaps it is not so much a case of who is in control, but whether the different sectors and providers have effective strategies for policy and planning, co-ordination and co-operation. New strategies and philosophies will be needed to prevent further fragmentation caused by shrinking budgets and competing initiatives. We have seen how further tensions have been created by successive educational reforms, particularly the local management of schools, moves towards opting out and grant-maintained status.

Another important issue is whether the Children Act will have any impact on the quality of provision. The inspection and registration processes are of limited use other than as a basic mechanism for ensuring minimum standards if they are not linked to training, advisory and curriculum development strategies. In view of the research findings about the effectiveness of pre-school provision, the quality of educational input must be a feature of the quality criteria for all settings. However, the task of defining and measuring quality is fraught with difficulties. Local authorities will need further support and guidance in this process, drawing on educational theory, research and practice. In terms of the educational quality of provision, the wider involvement of teachers and the educational advisory service would seem to be fruitful, as recommended by the Rumbold Report (DES, 1990).

The enterprise culture and a free-market approach to the

under-fives clearly does not work. In fact, as we have seen, there is a mixed market which creates divisions between those who can afford to pay or have employer-subsidized provision; those who cannot afford to pay and make do with the minimum available or do without; and those who can access publicly funded provision on the basis of defined need. Issues of quantity, quality, access and accessibility are not adequately addressed by the prevailing ethos. Children enter compulsory schooling with widely different experiences and backgrounds. Research has shown that this impacts in different ways on their potential, their performance in school and later life chances. Until more is done to improve provision and services for the under-fives on a comprehensive scale, inequity and inequality will be perpetuated from the first years of a child's life.

If this seems like more frustrated pessimism, it is a reflection of the complex task of sorting out the under-fives muddle. Looking at practice, the joint issues of training and developing the curriculum are of pressing concern. The debate about training is ongoing, with different proposals and possibilities being explored. As noted earlier, developments in National Vocational Qualifications offer a framework for progression for all adults who work with the under-fives. However, will this be adequate to future needs and will it reinforce a lower level of training, eventually removing early childhood specialists from degree and post-graduate level qualifications? This would be an ill-advised course for several reasons.

Early years teachers fulfil an important role in nursery and primary education. They act as advocates for young children; develop continuity between phases; provide valuable curriculum support and advice to teachers of older children; and, in managerial positions, can exert a positive influence on developing an 'early years up' rather than a 'top-down' perspective on curriculum development. Potentially, they can fulfil wider advisory roles in other forms of provision. Research has shown that the better educated the adults, the better educated the children. There is no evidence to suggest that the younger the child, the lower the level of expertise needed. Learning and teaching are complex processes demanding adequate levels of knowledge, understanding and skills, whatever the age group. In 1993 I attended a seminar organized by the European Community with early childhood specialists from the member states. Many were genuinely aghast at the proposals to downgrade the status and training of early years teachers through the 'Mum's Army' initiative particularly at a time when many European countries are moving towards better co-ordinated training with opportunities for progression and improved status (David, 1993b).

Of course, the content and rigour of a broad spectrum of courses need to be addressed. Broadly speaking, multiprofessional, inter-agency training seems to be an imperative. Understanding child development is not enough, since it does not provide an adequate foundation for educating young children. Adults need knowledge and understanding of the teaching and learning processes, how to develop appropriate contexts, strategies and interactions which stimulate learning and development and subject-matter knowledge. They need a wider view of equal opportunities, strategies for identifying and coping with child abuse, understanding roles and responsibilities and fostering good working relationships with children and adults. In order to understand children, they need to understand themselves, particularly their own values, attitudes and beliefs and how these impact on the curriculum.

In terms of the curriculum offered to the under-fives we have seen that certain key features contribute to the effectiveness of early education. These can and should be replicated in all different settings, according to the age and needs of the children. They need provision which acknowledges the importance of early learning, provides stimulation and challenge and an appropriate synthesis of care and education. Children need adults who are interested and interesting. Benign, inadequate environments where adults hold deficit views of children and their families deny human potential.

We know that there are now strong imperatives for change, but at the same time know the scale of changes that are needed. A pessimistic but realistic view acknowledges the obstacles to change.

However, some examples of recent developments and innovations in the field justify cautious optimism. These include:

- strategies for developing co-operation, consultation and co-ordination;
- the development of early years policies encompassing all under-fives provision;
- equal-opportunities policies and monitoring;
- joint-funding initiatives between local authorities, employers and parents;
- strategies for the involvement of the business sector;
- wider dissemination of information to the public about services and provision;
- the development of multi-agency, inter-disciplinary training;
- the appointment of training groups;
- better in-service training for teachers and nursery nurses;
- appointing teachers to Social Services day care and family centres;
- better liaison with infant and primary schools;
- extended day provision.

An innovative scheme in South Wales which opened in 1993 exemplifies what can be achieved with imagination, commitment and resources. A new family centre and primary school combines a nursery, day-care facilities for local families in need of help, a joint staffroom to encourage contact between social workers and teachers, a family therapy suite and pre- and after-school care. The centre can be used as a base for child minders and playgroups and will offer a range of family-support services (*TES*, 1.10.93).

Keeping the under-fives high on the political agenda demands more than commitment and resources. It demands a shift in values as well as in policies and practices. In the UK, children under 5 seem to have a lower priority than anywhere else in Europe. Currently responsibility for them is passed variously between parents, employers and the state.

In fact, all have an interest and a role to play. All have duties and responsibilities to young children. This is not just a question of politics and economics, but of ideology and respect for children's rights. There is a perverse irony in the Home Office funding for an experimental nursery-education programme based on the Highscope curriculum to combat rising juvenile crime and delinquency. Educating the under-fives must be seen as an issue in its own right and not just be left hanging on to the coat-tails of equal opportunities, the crime rate and the needs of the economy.

High-quality provision can and does make a difference to children, their families and teachers in later phases of schooling. It changes attitudes, aspirations and expectations. It cannot tackle all the inequalities in society, but educating the under-fives can make a difference, especially if anti-sexist, anti-racist and anti-discriminatory practices are adopted. This enables all children to develop positive self-images and a sense of their own capabilities and worth. Educating the under-fives matters to children in their early years and in their future lives. It matters to society because children are our future.

BIBLIOGRAPHY

Anning, A. (1991) *The First Years at School* (Buckingham: OUP).

Athey, C. (1990) *Extending Thought in Young Children: A Parent Teacher Partnership* (London: Paul Chapman Press).

Bennett, N. and Kell, J. (1989) *A Good Start? Four Year Olds in Infant Schools* (Oxford: Blackwell).

Board of Education (1933) *Report of the Consultative Committee on Infant and Nursery Schools* (Hadow Report) (London: HMSO).

Braun, D. (1992) 'Working with parents' in G. Pugh (ed.), *Contemporary Issues in the Early Years: Working Collaboratively for Children* (London: Paul Chapman and NCB).

Brown, M. (1990) *The High/Scope Approach to the National Curriculum* (High/Scope UK).

Bruce, T. (1987) *Early Childhood Education* (London: Hodder and Stoughton).

Central Advisory Council for Education (1967) *Children and Their Primary Schools* (Plowden Report) (London: HMSO).

Clark, M. M. (1988) *Children under Five: Educational Research and Evidence* (London: Gordon and Breach).

Cleave, S. and Brown, S. (1991) *Early to School: Four Year Olds in Infant Classes* (Slough: NFER/Nelson).

Commission on Social Justice (1993) *The Justice Gap and Social Justice in a Changing World* (London: Institute of Public Policy Research).

Curtis, A. (1986) *A Curriculum for the Pre-School Child* (Windsor: NFER).

David, T. (1990) *Under Five – Under Educated* (Buckingham: OUP).

David, T. (1993a) *Child Protection and the Early Years Teacher: Coping with Child Abuse* (Buckingham: OUP).

David, T. (1993b) *Educational Provision for Our Youngest Children: European Perspectives* (London: Paul Chapman Press).

DES (1978) *Special Educational Needs* (Warnock Report) (London: HMSO).

DES (1985) *The Curriculum from 5–16: Curriculum Matters 2* (London: HMSO).

DES (1989) *Aspects of Primary Education. The Education of Children under Five* (London: HMSO).

DES (1991) *Starting with Quality. Report of the Committee of Inquiry into the Quality of Educational Experiences Offered to 3- and 4-Year-Olds* (Rumbold Report). (London: HMSO).

DES (1993) *Statistical Bulletin on Under-Fives Education in England 11/93* (London: HMSO).

Department of Health (1991) *An Introduction to the Children Act* (London: HMSO).

Department of Health (1991) *The Children Act: Guidance and Regulations. Volume 2. Family Support, Day Care and Educational Provision for Young Children* (London: HMSO).

Dowling, M. (1992) (2nd edition) *Education 3–5* (London: Paul Chapman Press).

Drummond, M. J. (1993) *Assessing Children's Learning* (London: David Fulton).

Drummond, M. J., Lally, M., and Pugh, G. (1989) *Working with Children: Developing a Curriculum for the Early Years* (Nottingham: NES/NCB).

Ferri, E. (1992) *What Makes Childminding Work? A Study of Training for Childminders* (London: National Children's Bureau).

Ferri, E., Birchall, D., Gingell, V. and Gipps, C. (1981) *Combined Nursery Centres: A New Approach to Education and Day Care* (London: Macmillan).

Garland, C. and White, S. (1980) *Children and Day Nurseries* (London: Grant McIntyre).

Godenir, A. and Crahay, M. (1993) *The Role of Preschool Education in the Fight Against Failure at School: The Contribution of Scientific Research.* Report prepared for the Task Force (Commission of European Communities) (Belgium: University of Liege).

Gulbenkian Foundation (1993) *One Scandal Too Many. The Case for Comprehensive Protection for Children in All Settings.*

Harben, H. D. (1910) *The Endowment of Motherhood* (London: Fabian Tract 49).

Hennessy, E., Martin, S., Moss, P. and Melhuish, E. (1992) *Children and Day Care: Lessons from Research* (London: Paul Chapman Press).

Hohmann, M., Banet, B. and Weikart, D. P. (1979) *Young Children in Action* (Ypsilanti, MI: High/Scope Press).

House of Commons Select Committee Education, Science and Arts

Committee (1988) *Educational Provision for the Under Fives* (ESAC Report) (London: HMSO).

Moss, P. and Melhuish, E. (eds) (1991) *Current Issues in Day Care for Young Children: Research and Policy Implications* (London: Thomas Coram Research Institute).

Moyles, J. (1989) *Just Playing? The Role and Status of Play in Early Childhood Education* (Buckingham: OUP).

National Children's Bureau (1991) *Young Children in Group Day Care. Guidelines for Good Practice* (London: NCB).

National Commission on Education (1993) *Learning to Succeed* (London: Heinemann).

Osborn, A. F. and Millbank, J. E. (1989) *The Effects of Early Education* (Oxford: Clarendon Press).

Parry, M. and Archer, H. (1974) *Pre-school Education*, Schools Council Research Studies (London: Macmillan).

Penn, H. and Riley, K. A. (1992) *Managing Services for the Under Fives* (Harlow: Longman).

Powell, D. R. (1991) 'Parents and programs: early childhood as a pioneer in parent involvement and support', in S. L. Kagan (ed.) *The Care and Education of America's Young Children: Obstacles and Opportunities* (Illinois: University of Chicago Press).

Pugh, G. (1987) 'Portage in perspective: parental involvement in pre-school programmes', in A. Cohen (ed.), *Early Education: The Parents' Role* (London: Paul Chapman Press).

Pugh, G. (1988) *Services for the Under Fives. Developing a Co-ordinated Approach* (London: NCB).

Pugh, G. (1992) (ed.) *Contemporary Issues in the Early Years. Working Collaboratively for Children* (London: Paul Chapman Press and NCB).

Rouse, D. and Griffin, S. (1992) 'Quality for the under threes', in G. Pugh (ed.), *Contemporary Issues in the Early Years. Working Collaboratively for Children* (London: Paul Chapman Press and NCB).

Shorrocks, D. (1992) 'Evaluating Key Stage 1 assessments: the testing time of May, 1991', *Early Years*, 13(1).

Siraj-Blatchford, I. (1992) 'Why understanding cultural differences is not enough', in G. Pugh (ed.), *Contemporary Issues in the Early Years. Working Collaboratively for Children* (London: Paul Chapman Press and NCB).

Smith, E. A. (1992) 'Theory and practice in nursery education'. Unpublished M.Ed. thesis, University of Leeds.

Steedman, C. (1990) *Childhood, Culture and Class in Britain. Margaret McMillan 1860–1931* (London: Virago Press).

Times Educational Supplement 'Gathering the family under one roof', 1 October 1993.

Tizard, B. and Hughes, M. (1984) *Young Children Learning. Talking and Thinking at Home and in School* (London: Fontana).

Van der Eyken, W. (1967) *The Preschool Years* (Harmondsworth: Penguin).

Whitbread, N. (1972) *The Evolution of the Nursery and Infant School* (London: RKP).

Zigler, E. (1991) 'Using research to inform policy: the case of early intervention', in S. L. Kagan (ed.), *The Care and Education of America's Young Children: Obstacles and Opportunities* (Illinois: University of Chicago Press).

APPENDIX

Some useful addresses of organizations concerned with early childhood education.

British Association for Early Childhood Education (BAECE)
111 City View House
463 Bethnal Green Road
London E2 9QY

National Children's Bureau Early Childhood Unit
8 Wakley Street
London EC1V 7QE

National Play Information Centre
359–361 Euston Road
London NW1 3AL

Organisation Mondiale pour l'Education Préscolaire (OMEP)
UK Branch
c/o The Hon Secretary
144 Eltham Road
London SE9 5LW

Voluntary Organisation Liaison Council for Under Five's (VOLCUF)
77 Holloway Road
London N7 8JZ

INDEX

after-school clubs   19, 29
Anning, A.   5, 72, 80
Area Health Authorities   18
Archer, H.   12
Association of Metropolitan
   Authorities   13
Athey, C.   94, 95

Banet, B.   91
Bennett, N.   16
Birchall, D.   24
Board of Education   4
Board of Education Consultative
   Committee (Hadow
   Report)   5, 6, 7
Booth, Charles   3
Braun, D.   73, 77
Bowlby, John   7
Brown, M.   92
Brown, S.   16
Bruce, T.   5, 80
Bruner, Jerome   93

Central Advisory Council for
   Education (Plowden
   Report)   8
child development   63–5, 86,
   87, 94, 109
Child Health and Education
   Study   66
Clark, M.   65, 70
Children Act (1989)   14, 15, 16,
   17, 33, 51, 60, 62, 106
   adult–child ratios   19–29

impact on quality   107
recommendations and
   implications   36–44
registration and inspection
   36, 107
review duty   52, 53
review process   52
review reports   54–7
child development   63–5, 86,
   87, 94, 109
childminders   9, 27, 52, 71, 85
children's learning   75, 100–5
   home–school links   78
Cleave, S.   16
Commission on Social Justice
   59
Consortium for Longitudinal
   Studies   67
Crahay, M.   66, 69
curriculum
   assessment and evaluation
      85
   attitudes and beliefs   109
   balance   103
   content   86
   definition   80–2
   differentiation   84
   for children under three   99
   Highscope   68, 69, 91–3
   models   88–100
   organization   84
   planning   83
   progression   84
   quality criteria   104, 105
   structure   82
   subject disciplines   104

Curtis, A. 90

David, T. 49, 72, 109
Department of Education and
    Science (DES) 11, 14, 20,
    26, 32, 33, 75, 89, 107
Department for Education
    (DfE) 18, 107
Department of Health 12, 13,
    18, 24, 34, 44
Dowling, M. 77
Drummond, M. J. 81, 85, 96

Education Act (1870) 3
Education Act (1918) 6
Education Act (1944) 7
Education Reform Act (1988)
    16, 41, 42, 44
Education, Science and Arts
    Committee (ESAC) 10,
    13, 26, 33, 42
employers
    Employers For Childcare 58
    provision of childcare 58
    and joint funding initiatives
    107
equal opportunities 30, 51, 53,
    55, 70, 82, 83, 88, 100, 110,
    111

Fabian Society 4, 60
Ferri, E. 24, 71
Froebel, Friedrich 5, 63, 64

Garland, C. 8
Gingell, V. 24
Gipps, C. 24

Godenir, A. 66, 69
Griffin, S. 81
Gulbenkian Foundation 59

Harben, H. D. 4
Hennessy, E. 66, 67, 74
Her Majesty's Inspectorate
    (HMI) 88, 100
Hohmann, M. 91
Highscope curriculum 68, 69,
    91–3, 111
Hughes, M. 78

Isaacs, Susan 4, 5, 64, 80

Kell, J. 16

Lally, M. 81
leisure departments 18, 29
local authorities 14, 15, 18,
    37–9, 54, 106
    combined centres 19, 23
    curriculum guidelines 87,
    100
    day nurseries 9, 19, 22, 60,
    66, 110
    family centres 19, 23, 110
    family support services 19,
    24, 79
    Portage 19, 24, 25
local education authorities
    (LEAs) 12, 13, 18, 23, 24,
    34
    Bradford 55
    Bromley, London Borough
    of 20
    Cheshire 55

local education authorities
(*cont'd*)
Cleveland 20, 55
Devon 55
Dorset 20
Gloucestershire 20, 55
Havering, London Borough
of 20
Lancashire 56
Leeds 55
Lewisham, London Borough
of 69
Liverpool 69
Manchester 20, 55
Merton, London Borough of
20
Newham, London Borough
of 20
North Tyneside 69
Oldham 69
Sheffield 55
Wolverhampton 20
Local Management of Schools
(LMS) 16, 43

McMillan, Margaret 4, 5, 6,
64, 80
McMillan, Rachel 4
Major, John 61
Martin, S. 66, 67, 74
Melhuish, E. C. 35, 66, 67, 74
Milbank, J. E. 30, 66, 68
Montessori, Maria 4, 5, 64, 80
Moser, Sir Claus 60
Moss, P. 35, 66, 67, 74
Moyles, J. 101

nannies 19, 28

National Children's Bureau
11, 99
National Childminders
Association 27
National Commission on
Education 51, 60, 61
National Curriculum 10, 21,
41, 89, 97, 98, 104
nursery schools and classes 9,
19, 20, 42, 43, 66, 76, 77

Osborn, A. F. 30, 66, 68
Owen, Robert 2, 3

parents
and childrearing 48–50
as partners 75–9
educative role of 71
involvement in pre-school
settings 76
lone 46, 47
lone-parent organizations 52
pressure groups 62
and toddler groups 19, 26
Parry, M. 12
Patten, John 42
Paul Hamlyn Foundation 60
Penn, H. 19, 31, 40
Perry Pre-school Project 68
Piaget, Jean 68, 91
play 74, 75, 78, 83, 84, 89, 94,
95, 97, 98, 100–3
playgroups 19, 25, 60, 66
Powell, D. R. 76
Portage 19, 24, 25
pre-school education
effects and effectiveness 64,
109
research background 65–70

Pre-school Playgroups
     Association (PPA)   25, 26,
     52, 76
private nurseries   9, 19, 28
Project Head Start   67
Pugh, G.   12, 48, 76, 77, 81

qualifications, for under-fives
     workers   22, 23, 27, 28, 32

ratios, adult–child   21–3, 27,
     28
Riley, K.   19, 31, 40
Rouse, D.   81
Rowntree, Seebohm   3
Rumbold Report   14, 16, 26, 32,
     33, 40, 42, 89, 107

schemas   91, 94–6
schematic approach   94
Siraj-Blatchford, I.   30
Shorrocks, D.   104
Smith, E. A.   40, 74

Social Services departments
     (SSD)   12, 13, 18, 22, 23,
     24, 34, 36, 44
special educational needs
     24–6, 31, 38, 39, 44, 53, 56,
     57, 76, 82, 83, 84, 88, 96
special schools   24
Steedman, C.   5
Steiner, Rudolf   5, 80

Thatcher, Margaret   59
Tizard, B.   78
toy libraries   19, 29

Van der Eyken, W.   49
Vygotsky, Lev   93

Warnock Report   31
Weikart, D.   91
Whitbread, N.   3, 6, 7
White, S.   8
workplace nurseries   9, 19, 28

Zigler, E.   70